# HARNESS NEGATIVE THINKING

## SEVEN STEPS TO TURN SELF-DOUBT INTO SUCCESS WITHOUT TOXIC POSITIVITY

JOSEPH VALE

# CONTENTS

# BEFORE YOU TURN TO THE NEXT PAGE
## I'VE GOT A GIFT FOR YOU.

As a thank-you for picking up this book, I want to give you something extra:
The Harness Negative Thinking Workbook — completely FREE.

It's my way of helping you turn insight into action.
Inside, you'll find simple exercises, thought-reframe prompts, and reflection tools to help you apply what you've just read in real life.

No fluff. No overwhelm: Just practical guidance to help you move forward with clarity and confidence.

https://harnessgrowthpress.aweb.page

# INTRODUCTION

We often despise negative thoughts and struggle so much to get rid of them as much as possible. That fight becomes exhausting when we keep noticing that the same thoughts dominate our minds despite our attempts to think positively. This made me wonder if there was an effective way to handle negative thoughts other than forcing ourselves to think positively. This book is about to reveal the secret trick to liberating ourselves from the bondage of believing the worst about ourselves and others.

It might sound counterintuitive, but the great news is that the very negative thoughts and self-doubt we wrestle with can be used to guide us toward understanding great revelations of what we are capable of! Those nagging negative thoughts can secretly nudge you toward unlocking an enriched life bursting with your true potential. All we need to have is a change in perspective! Intriguing, right? But how does this work, you might wonder? *Instead of choosing to believe our negative thoughts, we can decide to believe the very opposite of every negative thought we have!* Imagine what would happen if we consciously chose to accept the very opposite of what our negative thoughts are saying!

For instance, if your mind is telling you that you can never learn a new skill, choose to see that as life beautifully revealing to you what you actually can do! Why? Because fear is always false evidence appearing real! This means, of course, that you can learn any new skill you choose to. We only have to understand how our brains are wired to fear change. So, just because our minds interpret certain things as threats when they're actually not, doesn't mean we should believe them!

We have all been there—running away from our fears and convincing ourselves that suppressing negativity is the way to live. But what if there's a different path, a more authentic road where negativity doesn't hold power over us but fuels our growth?

Instead of allowing these doubts to dictate our lives, consider flipping them on their head. For every negative whisper, we could choose to embrace the polar opposite. That kernel of doubt screaming "You're not good enough"? How about challenging it by affirming that you're more than enough? What might happen then? Could it be that within the cacophony of negativity lies a clue to your vast capabilities waiting to be unraveled? By embracing this mindset shift, we're not just surviving but thriving, harvesting remarkable growth in unexpected places.

You are probably nodding along because it feels logical, right? It's a good thing you picked up this book because that's exactly the kind of reasoned decision-making rooted in self-awareness you are about to be skilled at. We're diving into something truly fresh here—transforming negativity into actionable steps for real success. This isn't another attempt to bury your emotions under a mountain of unquestioning optimism. Nope. This is about authenticity and balance, finding strength in our flaws and courage in our fears.

Let me share a personal story to give you a little background. Growing up in the bustling streets of New York City, I found myself tangled in high expectations and constant self-doubt. Ever felt the weight of trying to meet unrealistic standards day after day? Perfectionism quietly crept into my life, fueled by toxic positivity that insisted on constant smiles even when things were crumbling inside. Sound familiar?

But here's where it gets interesting. Instead of getting lost in that whirlwind, I decided to pause and take stock. What was driving those feelings? Was it really just about being perfect, or was there something deeper? It turns out that by acknowledging my negativity, I stumbled upon a powerful realization—it wasn't my enemy but a misunderstood ally. The moment I stopped battling against it, breakthroughs started to unfold. I began exploring mental health strategies and channeling my experiences into understanding how negativity, when harnessed properly, could propel us forward rather than pull us down.

Over time, I had the privilege of working with diverse groups—professionals, students, and creatives—each wrestling with their own brand of self-doubt. Through countless conversations and explorations, one glaring gap emerged within traditional self-help narratives: the suppression of negative emotions. Everywhere I looked, people were taught to shove aside their worries rather than learn from them. And there it was, the missing link that many failed to see—a chance to rewrite the script and genuinely grow by embracing our inner struggles.

Out of this realization grew my debut book, *Harness Negative Thinking: 7 Steps to Turn Self-Doubt Into Success Without Toxic Positivity*. It's packed with practical advice woven through personal tales like mine, offering a relatable and empowering way to sidestep outdated self-help norms. Here, you'll find a realistic path to personal growth by fully embracing, rather than dodging, those inner battles you think are holding you back.

So, are you ready to uncover new possibilities? Just take a moment to envision the freedom of living authentically, where negativity doesn't limit your journey but enriches it. What if we dared to embrace those shadows instead of running from them? Is it possible that therein lies the catalyst for change, waiting patiently to be acknowledged?

Let's explore this new perspective together, hand in hand. It's going to be a high-energy ride full of love, warmth, and empathy. More importantly, it's about daring to question conventional wisdom and stepping into a space of genuine empowerment. Are you curious to see what's possible when we stop fearing our thoughts and start listening to them?

Let's engage openly, share honestly, and discover warm-hearted, engaging insights that dare us to grow. After all, we have only this one life, so why not make it our best and most fulfilling adventure yet? There's so much to uncover, and the journey begins now. Ready to start this life-changing exploration? Let's do it together, with open minds and brave hearts!

# STEP 1: IDENTIFY AND ACKNOWLEDGE NEGATIVE THOUGHTS

Being aware of and acknowledging our negative thoughts can fundamentally help us manage the landscape of our emotions. It might seem counterintuitive in a world that promotes relentless positivity, but understanding our darker emotions is where personal growth often begins. We become more self-aware when we open ourselves up to these hidden parts of our psyche. This chapter dares you to face what's often ignored: those whispers of doubt or fears that lurk beneath the surface.

Now, it's time for us to explore why society tends to shy away from negativity and how this avoidance can impact us. Let's think about the role negative thoughts play in shaping our mindset and how failure to acknowledge them might manifest in our daily lives. Together, we will look at different techniques for identifying these thoughts. Sometimes, we find ourselves responding to life in ways that worsen situations. However, we can beat this problem by improving our awareness. Knowing our negative thoughts and mastering different ways to manage ourselves better can help us take control of our responses and interactions with others. As you read on, you'll see why embracing both the positive and negative aspects of your emotional spectrum is necessary not only for your individual well-being but also for creating stronger connections with those around you.

## WHY WE AVOID NEGATIVE THOUGHTS

In today's world, where social media bombards us with perfect life snapshots and motivational quotes, have you ever noticed that there's a persistent stigma attached to acknowledging negative emotions? We're often encouraged to put on a brave face and focus solely on the positive. This can make it difficult for us to express our true feelings, leading us to suppress negativity instead. *Society's preference for positivity over honesty has created an unrealistic expectation that we must always be happy, upbeat, and untroubled.* However, this mindset doesn't allow us to fully engage with and understand the full spectrum of human emotions. Toxic positivity is the idea of denying our negative thoughts and feelings instead of constructively addressing them.

### The Impact of Suppressing Negative Emotions and Thoughts

Suppressing negative thoughts may seem like a short-term solution to maintaining sanity in our hectic daily lives. After all, nobody wants to dwell on things that evoke discomfort or pain. However, when we continuously push aside these feelings, they don't simply disappear; they fester beneath the surface. This unresolved emotional baggage can significantly contribute to increased fear and self-doubt. When we ignore our negative thoughts, they tend to manifest in other areas of our lives. For instance, work-related anxiety might seep into personal relationships, creating tension and misunderstandings. Without addressing the root causes of these feelings, self-doubt flourishes, undermining confidence and self-esteem. The vicious cycle of unacknowledged negativity continues to build, further entrenching us in a state of perpetual unease.

Many people turn to distraction as a means to escape negativity. Binge-watching TV shows, aimlessly scrolling through social media feeds, or diving into endless online shopping are common ways to divert attention from uncomfortable thoughts. These activities can offer a temporary pause from reality, but they're just that—temporary. It's similar to putting a bandage on a wound without cleaning it first. The relief is momentary; once the distraction ends, those suppressed feelings rush back with even greater intensity. This cycle often leads to an ongoing struggle with procrastination and avoidance, preventing any real progress toward emotional well-being.

## HOW DENYING OUR NEGATIVE EMOTIONS AND THOUGHTS AFFECTS US

Denial is a way to deal with negative thoughts by pretending certain feelings or situations don't exist, thinking this will help us avoid pain. However, denial is a weak defense mechanism that creates a fake sense of safety, pulling you away from your genuine feelings and experiences. For example, you might say everything is okay at work during a tough time, ignoring signs of stress until you reach a breaking point. Denial just puts problems off, making them worse when they finally come up. You may not see that denying your feelings can make you emotionally numb. You stop feeling a full range of emotions, both good and bad, so joy can feel less vibrant. Relationships can struggle because real connections need openness. When you hide your true feelings, trust can fade between friends or partners. If you deny your emotions, you might try to avoid them by distracting yourself with activities or substances, leading to addiction or unhealthy coping methods that create even more problems (Raypole, 2020).

- **Effect on health:** Denying feelings can also hurt your physical health. Stress builds up in your body if not addressed, leading to headaches, stomach issues, or heart problems. It's like your body is always tense from hidden emotions. Sleep problems can happen too, with anxious thoughts keeping you awake. The more you deny your feelings, the harder it can become to find peace, causing ongoing tiredness and lethargy.

- **Effect on work:** Denial makes teamwork difficult in the workplace. If a colleague refuses to talk about real worries about a project, it can slow down the group. Hidden frustrations can emerge in unhelpful ways during meetings, leading to conflict and poor communication. When everyone pretends problems don't exist, the team may struggle to tackle issues together.

- **Effect on decision-making:** Denying feelings can also affect your decision-making. You might make choices without truly considering your feelings, leading to regrets later. For example, you may take a job just to leave a bad situation, only to find new challenges there. Quick decisions often come from not facing what's really bothering you, clouding your judgment.

- **Effect on mental health:** Over time, denial can harm your mental health. Thought patterns can become rigid, making it hard for you to adapt to changes and causing frustration. Being in denial makes it harder to be resilient. When facing tough situations, you can feel overwhelmed and believe you can't handle things. The more you avoid your feelings, the more difficult challenges appear.

- **Effect on social life:** Socially, you can become isolated if you deny your feelings. Friends may distance themselves if they sense something is wrong, but you won't talk. This creates a lonely environment. The irony is that reaching out for support can be the first step toward healing, which you often overlook. Attending social events can feel overwhelming because of the fake emotional front you keep up, reinforcing a cycle of loneliness.

- **Effect on self-esteem:** Denial has an effect on your self-esteem. When you don't acknowledge your pain, you might feel unworthy of support and engage in negative self-talk. You may feel you should manage your problems alone, which can worsen feelings of inadequacy. This cycle distorts your self-image and makes asking for help feel like a weakness.

- **Effect on life goals:** Denial can also affect your life goals. When you ignore negative emotions, you might drift from your passions. Your dreams can fade as you focus solely on getting by rather than finding fulfillment. The path to understanding yourself becomes unclear. Each time you push down frustration or sadness, you move further away from your true self.

- **Effect on relationships:** In relationships, communication can suffer when you deny your feelings. Important talks about feelings and goals are avoided, leading to hidden issues. A false front of happiness can mask deeper problems, creating resentment. When your partner feels ignored, they may withdraw, thinking their needs won't be met. Over time, this can break down trust. Emotional events can trigger old pain that's often ignored. For instance, if you have faced loss, you might push down your grief, thinking you're handling it well. Yet, special dates or reminders can bring up deep sadness. Denial doesn't erase these feelings; it just delays them. Eventually, hiding grief can lead to sudden emotional outbursts or sadness at unexpected times.

- **Effect on others:** The effect of denial can carry over generations. Children observe their parents' emotional responses. If a parent often denies their feelings, you might learn to do the same, missing out on healthy emotional expression. Breaking this cycle takes effort and self-awareness, which can be hard when you're stuck in denial because you may not realize the pattern.

- **Effect on creativity:** Denial can also stifle your creativity. Artistic expression often comes from real emotions; when those are suppressed, creativity can dry up. When caught in denial, writers, musicians, and artists like you might struggle to create. The spark that fuels creativity dims when you avoid exploring your feelings. Finding new ideas often relies on understanding and accepting your emotions.
- **Effect on emotional well-being:** Denying emotions can create feelings of shame and guilt. You might believe you should cope better or that your pain isn't valid. This emotional burden can build up, leading to a sense of being trapped. Society often values strength, which can discourage showing vulnerability. The idea that you must always "stay strong" can keep you stuck in denial.

Facing your emotions openly can seem scary but can lead to personal growth. Tackling your fears and insecurities often brings understanding and enlightenment. Accepting your feelings allows you to process your experiences, promoting healing. Working through emotions can restore hope and improve your relationships. While it may be tough, taking small, purposeful steps can help you embrace your feelings. This is important for taking back control of your life and well-being, leading to richer experiences and more authentic connections.

## THE IMPACT OF ESCAPING FROM OUR NEGATIVE EMOTIONS AND THOUGHTS

Escapism represents yet another approach to keeping negativity at bay. This can take various forms, such as immersing oneself in fantasy novels, video games, or incessant travel. While these activities can provide respite, they often act as temporary shelters rather than solutions. Engaging in escapism allows us to step away from harsh realities momentarily. Nevertheless, without confronting the issues head-on, they merely accumulate more unresolved emotional burdens. Once the comforting cocoon of escapism fades, we find ourselves right back where we started, facing the same daunting negative thoughts.

When we take an honest look at why society avoids discussing negativity, it's clear that much of this hesitance stems from a misunderstanding of emotional health. Emotions aren't inherently good or bad—they're simply signals that something requires our attention. Acknowledging this perspective helps us grow personally. Being aware of and processing our negative thoughts can help us achieve genuine happiness. However, when we only focus on the positive, we miss opportunities to address underlying issues.

Moreover, understanding our negative emotions can help create stronger connections with others. When we share our vulnerabilities honestly, we encourage authentic communication, and this openness can deepen our relationships by promoting empathy and trust. Everyone faces challenges, and accepting this universal truth can empower us to tackle negativity with patience and compassion.

## THE IMPORTANCE OF AWARENESS

Have you ever wondered where all our negativity comes from? It's necessary to know why we think the way we do; after all, you can't heal what you don't understand. Thus, being aware of negativity entails a deeper understanding of your feelings and mindset. This awareness encourages you to identify negative thoughts, which can help you understand what really affects you. When you dig deeper into your thoughts, you can discover areas of your life that may need change or improvement. Think of this process like peeling an onion; sometimes, the core issues are hidden beneath layers of everyday life.

Until you actively look for these problems, they may remain unnoticed.

### Use Journaling to Improve Your Self-Awareness

Writing down your thoughts and feelings regularly creates a written record that makes it easier to identify repeating patterns of negativity. For example, you might notice that you often worry about your skills at work or your relationships with friends. Understanding these patterns allows you to spot negative thoughts before they take over your mind. Instead of reacting to these feelings only when they become overwhelming, you can confront them early. Journaling offers a private space for introspection, helping you filter through the chaos and focus on what truly matters in your life.

### Taking Control of Responses

The awareness gained from recognizing negative thoughts lets you take charge of how you respond to situations. Have you ever found yourself reacting in fear or anxiety without knowing why? This often happens when unexamined fears influence your behavior from the background. That's why as you shine a light on these fears, you empower yourself to choose how to act instead of simply reacting out of habit. This change is freeing; it allows you to align your actions with your values and goals instead of reacting impulsively due to fear.

### Challenging Inadequacies

Let's consider a specific example: a person who feels inadequate at work might not realize that this feeling comes from a past failure. If they do not examine these thoughts, they may wrongly accept them as truth. However, by engaging in reflection, such as journaling, they can uncover that these feelings are linked to a past experience. With this newfound awareness, they can challenge these beliefs by reminding themselves of their achievements and strengths. This process reduces the hold that feelings of inadequacy have over their mental state.

### Improving Relationships

Being aware of negativity can also lead to healthier relationships. When you are conscious of your negative thoughts and their origins, you are less likely to project these feelings onto others. This awareness can transform how you interact with people. For instance, if you know that your irritability stems from stress, you can discuss this with friends or family instead of snapping at them. When you explain your feelings, you can avoid unnecessary arguments, which helps create a more understanding and supportive atmosphere.

### Constructive Awareness vs. Dwelling

Some people may worry that focusing on negative thoughts will only worsen them. It's important to differentiate between dwelling on negativity and being constructively aware of it. The latter means acknowledging negative thoughts without allowing them to define your whole story. Instead, you can use this awareness as a launchpad for better outcomes. Understanding the reasons behind your feelings can support healing and encourage growth rather than simply amplifying negativity.

Strengthening self-awareness enhances resilience. Life will always include obstacles and disappointments, but knowing how to handle negative thoughts helps you recover more effectively. You shift from being a passive victim of circumstances to an active participant in your own life. Equipped with insights about your thoughts and feelings, you create pathways for growth, turning challenges into opportunities for learning. This proactive approach not only aids personal development but also prepares you to tackle life's hurdles with confidence and strength.

## EMBRACING THE ROLE OF NEGATIVITY

Negativity is a universal experience we all face at various points in our lives. It's vital to recognize that negative thoughts and emotions aren't signs of failure or weakness. Instead, it is part of the shared human experience. From the moment we wake up to the time we go to bed, we might encounter countless situations that stir negative thoughts. Missing a deadline, receiving criticism, or even a minor inconvenience like spilling coffee can trigger them. It's comforting to know that we are not alone in this; everyone experiences negativity in their own unique way.

Accepting negativity as a natural part of life doesn't mean wallowing in self-pity or letting it take over our minds. Instead, it means noticing these thoughts and feelings for what they are: fleeting moments that don't define us. Embracing this mindset can be liberating. When you stop seeing negativity as an enemy, you open up space for learning and growth. Think of negativity as a cloudy day. Just as clouds eventually pass, so do negative thoughts.

Interestingly, some of the most successful people have turned their inner critics into catalysts for success. Consider Thomas Edison, who faced numerous failures before inventing the electric light bulb. He didn't allow the voice of negativity to halt his progress. Instead, he reframed failures as lessons, using them to drive innovation. Figures like Oprah Winfrey and Steve Jobs also faced setbacks and criticism but learned to use such negativity to fuel their determination.

The stories of these achievers highlight an essential truth: Negativity doesn't have to be a roadblock. It can be a launchpad. Transforming a nagging inner critic into motivation requires a shift in perspective. It's about listening to that critical voice and discerning which parts can help you improve. Are there aspects of your work or behavior that need adjustment? Accepting constructive criticism, whether from within or outside, can lead to substantial personal development.

Viewing negativity as a prompt for development means actively seeking growth opportunities in challenging situations. It's a bit like gardening. You sometimes need to prune away the dead leaves to grow healthy plants. Negative thoughts and experiences can act like those dead leaves, signaling areas that require attention and care. By addressing them, we promote healthier and more fruitful development.

For instance, when facing a setback, ask yourself what you can learn from the situation instead of dwelling on what went wrong. What strategies could prevent similar outcomes in the future? This reflective approach turns potential stumbling blocks into stepping stones. It cultivates resilience, paving the way for personal and professional growth.

Practical exercises can assist in harnessing negativity constructively. Here is a simple guideline worth considering: Keep a journal where you document recurring negative thoughts. This exercise not only makes you more aware of your patterns but also helps in tracking your progress over time. Regularly revisiting your entries can provide valuable insights into how you've evolved, reinforcing positivity amidst adversity. Reflect on your past responses to negative thoughts and determine what worked and what didn't. With practice, you'll get better at managing these moments, which turns our potential obstacles into opportunities for advancement.

## HARNESS YOUR NEGATIVE THOUGHTS FOR GROWTH

We've established that negative thoughts don't have to be your enemies. They're more like uninvited guests at a party—you might not want them there, but they can provide fresh perspectives if handled well. Let's take a closer look at how we can turn these gloomy thoughts into tools for self-improvement.

Self-reflecting on our negative thoughts can be a powerful tool for understanding our personal challenges and identifying areas where we can grow. It's like shining a spotlight on parts of ourselves that we might typically overlook. For example, many people experience self-doubt at some point in their lives. Instead of pushing those feelings aside, try to pause and take a closer look. What can these feelings teach you? Often, they reveal fears or insecurities. When we acknowledge these feelings, we can find a path toward meaningful change. For instance, if you feel anxious about giving a speech, this might point to a lack of confidence in your communication skills. Knowing that this anxiety opens up an opportunity for improvement allows you to build your capabilities in public speaking.

### Channeling Critical Feedback

Moreover, listening to the critical feedback we give ourselves can help us to set realistic goals. We often hear criticism from others, but the thoughts we have about ourselves can be even more impactful. It's easy to slide into self-criticism that lacks direction. However, what if you decided to use this inner dialogue constructively? Instead of viewing inner criticism purely as negative, think of it as a detailed map that shows where you can improve. For example, if you are trying to enhance your athletic performance and hear that inner voice suggesting you aren't training hard enough, this could be a push to create a training plan. This plan could challenge you while also being safe and manageable.

### Embracing Constructive Criticism

Embracing constructive criticism can also lead to innovation and creativity. This requires a shift in how we think about critiques. Instead of seeing them as attacks on our self-esteem, we can view them as sandpaper smoothing our rough edges. In creative areas like writing or art, feedback from critics often helps us to refine our work. The same idea applies to our internal dialogue. If there is something you want to create but your inner critic is shouting, "It's not good enough," use that criticism to make your work better. Maybe you need to rethink your approach or try out new techniques. Let the critique inspire you to find creative solutions.

### Interpreting Negative Thoughts

The real challenge—and opportunity—comes in learning how to interpret and handle these negative thoughts. Instead of allowing them to become roadblocks, think of them as signposts that can guide your journey. As shared before, meditation or journaling creates space for reflection and understanding. Writing down your thoughts lets you step back and notice patterns you might miss in a busy mind. Look for recurring themes in your negativity, as these could highlight areas of your life that need more attention. This recognition can help create a roadmap for positive action.

### Negativity Audit

Ready to hear what else you can use to better understand yourself? This strategy is to schedule regular "negativity audits." Set aside an hour each week to reflect on recent negative thoughts or feelings. During this time, ask yourself some important questions: What triggered these feelings? How did they affect you? Most importantly, what lessons can you draw from them? This practice is not about erasing negativity from your life but acknowledging it as a natural part of being human. Learning to live with these thoughts and understanding where they come from can help you grow.

In essence, the process of engaging with negative thoughts is not easy, but with time and practice, it can lead to substantial personal growth and a deeper understanding of oneself. Embrace these thoughts, use them to clarify your goals, and allow them to propel you toward positive outcomes.

## CREATE A BALANCED MINDSET

Balancing our thoughts can be compared to walking a tightrope. On one side are negative thoughts, and on the other, positive thoughts. Achieving this balance helps us deal with challenges more effectively. This means that whenever we face a problem, it's essential to look at it from different angles. If we focus only on the bright side, we may overlook important details that could lead us into trouble. On the other hand, if we let negative thoughts take over, we might miss out on potential solutions or opportunities.

Take a puzzle, for instance. If you only see it from one perspective, you might struggle to find how the pieces fit together. A broader view encourages creativity and provides a solid foundation for making decisions. Those who manage to consider both optimistic possibilities and realistic constraints usually find more comprehensive solutions. For instance, consider entrepreneurs; those who evaluate both market opportunities and potential risks are often the ones who turn their startups into successful businesses.

Life can be overwhelming with its challenges, and it's easy to feel weighed down. However, leaning too heavily on negative thinking can lead to self-doubt and fear. A balanced outlook helps you manage life's ups and downs more gracefully. Think of life as a boat journey. Positive thoughts keep us afloat, while acknowledging potential storms ahead prepares us for rough waters. Resilient individuals understand that setbacks are part of life and use them as stepping stones instead of stumbling blocks.

Take professional athletes as an example. They know injuries and losses are part of their journey. Rather than dwelling on these negatives, they accept them, learn from their experiences, and push for improvement. Building resilience doesn't mean ignoring failures but turning them into motivation for future success. This skill helps prevent setbacks from derailing us, allowing us to move forward even when times are tough.

### Know Your Strengths and Weaknesses

It's easy to concentrate only on what we do well, but ignoring our shortcomings can lead to complacency. Meanwhile, focusing too much on our faults may hinder progress. Acknowledging our limitations provides clarity on where we need to grow, and when we embrace who we are, including our imperfections, we lay the groundwork for genuine development.

Consider a musician. They know their instrument very well. They understand what they excel at and where they struggle. This awareness does not dishearten them; instead, it serves as a guide for their practice. When they actively address their weaknesses, they gradually become well-rounded performers. This principle can apply to many areas of life, including careers, relationships, and personal goals. Understanding our complete selves allows us to seek genuine improvement without falling into extremes.

## AVOIDING EXTREME THINKING

Acknowledging both strengths and weaknesses promotes personal growth and helps avoid the dangers of extreme thinking. Overly positive thinking can lead to unrealistic expectations, while excessive negativity can create hopelessness. Neither approach is healthy in the long run. The real power lies in the middle ground, where optimism energizes hope and realism brings clarity.

Take a look at the workplace. An overly optimistic leader might ignore warning signs, leading teams into unexpected challenges. On the other hand, a pessimistic manager might lower team morale, making it harder for people to innovate. Leaders who find the right balance between positivity and careful consideration build environments where creativity thrives, while caution ensures projects remain grounded.

Creating balanced thoughts takes mindfulness and practice. One simple start is to pay attention to your internal dialogue. Are you leaning more toward negativity or unchecked optimism? Reflecting on your thought patterns and adjusting them as needed can be very helpful. It's important to clarify that this doesn't mean suppressing your emotions or forcing yourself to feel positive. Instead, it's about being honest with yourself and responding thoughtfully.

Seek feedback from others, such as your friends or colleagues. They often notice things we might miss. When we invite their diverse perspectives, we can deepen our understanding and fine-tune our approach. This collaborative effort strengthens our ability to maintain a steady balance between positive and negative thoughts.

Life and our thoughts are both fluid; some days will be easier than others, and that's completely normal. The key is to keep reflecting and adjusting, making a continuous commitment to grow based on the reality of our experiences. Embracing this journey helps us maintain that delicate balance while managing life's many twists and turns.

## SUMMARY

As we wrap things up, it's clear that recognizing negative thoughts isn't about giving them the power to dictate our lives. Instead, by acknowledging them, we can turn these thoughts into stepping stones for personal growth. The chapter walked us through the different ways we often try to dodge negativity. Everyone experiences setbacks and uncertainties; what matters is how we handle them. So, let's embrace this path of self-discovery and growth, understanding that negativity is just one piece of a much larger puzzle. The next chapter will help us better manage our thoughts by learning how to separate facts from fiction.

# STEP 2: SEPARATE FACT FROM FICTION

Separating fact from fiction in our thoughts is a skill that can change how we view the world and ourselves. Every day, we're bombarded with information, emotions, and beliefs that can distort our reality. It's easy to fall into mental traps where exaggerations and assumptions cloud our judgment. However, noticing these patterns opens up a path to clarity. Just like cleaning out a dusty attic, sorting through what's true and what's not requires effort but brings peace of mind. When we hone this ability, we empower ourselves to make decisions based on reality rather than fear or misconceptions, setting a foundation for a more balanced life.

Have you wondered if what you are afraid of is really as bad as it looks in your mind? It's important to go through the process of questioning our minds and understanding their distortions. Thus, we will learn how cognitive distortions manifest and discuss techniques to identify them in our daily lives.

## WHAT ARE COGNITIVE DISTORTIONS?

But what are cognitive distortions? Let's find out: Sometimes, when we let our minds run wild, we create what are known as *cognitive distortions*. For instance, have you ever thought, *What if I fail?* Then your mind takes it further, suggesting you will never succeed at anything. These are irrational fears and exaggerated beliefs that can cloud our judgment and paralyze us. They often build a false narrative based on past experiences or negative self-talk. What if the worst-case scenario isn't as likely as it seems? When we examine these fears, we can often find they're rooted more in anxiety than reality. Have you noticed how a minor worry can grow into a massive wall that stops you in your tracks? That's why we need to shine some light on these fears and ask ourselves which parts are real and which parts are simply our minds playing tricks.

It's tempting to avoid what scares us, but in doing so, we miss out on growth and self-discovery. However, if we question our fears, we can understand them better. Instead of making assumptions about what might happen, we can test them. What if we approached our fears like scientists? We could gather evidence to see if the scary scenarios we imagine are actually likely to happen. Are you ready to have a more accurate perception of reality and be free from things you fear that might not even be real? The tools we are about to discuss will help us create a framework for separating truth from distortion. By the end of the chapter, you'll be equipped to face challenges with a mindset rooted in reality, minimizing self-doubt and embracing personal growth.

Cognitive distortions are patterns of thinking that can significantly affect how we view ourselves and our abilities. These mental traps distort our perceptions, often leading us away from the truth of our situations. Among the many types of cognitive distortions, two common ones are catastrophizing and all-or-nothing thinking. Let's now unpack more on what these distortions look like in everyday life situations.

### Catastrophizing

Catastrophizing involves imagining the worst possible scenario without considering any other outcomes. For example, if you mistakenly send an email to the wrong person at work, you might irrationally believe that this mistake could lead to losing your job. This kind of thinking can trigger feelings of stress and anxiety that may not be warranted.

Catastrophizing can create a cycle of negativity that makes it hard for us to move forward. Instead of seeing a situation as an opportunity to learn and grow, we fixate on the worst outcome and feel stuck. If we fail a test, for instance, we might think that we are failures in life and that we'll never succeed in our careers. This kind of thinking diminishes our confidence and keeps us from taking risks, like trying again or pursuing a new path in education or work. It's easy for us to spiral down into a dark place when we only focus on the worst-case scenarios.

Everyday situations can trigger this form of thinking in us. Let's say we are invited to a social gathering. Instead of feeling excitement, we start imagining all the ways it could go wrong—*what if no one talks to me? What if I embarrass myself?* Focusing on these fears can prevent us from enjoying the moment or making new friends. We may end up avoiding the party altogether, missing out on fun experiences that could enrich our lives, which is why the habit of catastrophizing always limits our opportunities and isolates us.

Catastrophizing often happens in our relationships, too. For example, if your partner takes a bit longer to reply to a text, you may panic and think they are losing interest or that something is wrong. This worry can escalate, leading you to confront them with anxiety instead of waiting for a reasonable explanation. When we jump to the worst conclusion, we risk damaging the relationship over a misunderstanding. This knee-jerk reaction can create tension and distrust, making it difficult for both of you to feel secure and happy.

But where does that habit come from? What causes it? The roots of catastrophizing often lie in our past experiences. If we have faced hardships, we may develop a habit of expecting the worst as a protective mechanism. While it is natural for us to want to guard ourselves against pain, this pattern becomes harmful. For example, if you have experienced a job loss before, you might constantly fear that any small mistake at work signals impending firing. Thus, rather than focusing on doing your best and improving, you may remain paralyzed by anxiety, which can affect your performance and relationships with coworkers.

How can we solve the problem of chronically expecting the worst? Mindfulness and self-reflection can help us catch those spiraling thoughts. When we notice ourselves jumping to worst-case scenarios, we can pause and challenge those thoughts. We can ask ourselves if there is evidence to support our fears or if we are imagining things that are unlikely to happen. Breaking the cycle of catastrophic thinking requires practice, but with time, thinking more rationally can become a habit.

Changing our self-talk is a critical strategy. Instead of saying, "I'll fail," we can reframe it as "I might need to prepare differently next time." Notice how this shift encourages growth instead of fear? Positive affirmations can also help reshape how we view challenges, turning what seems daunting into something achievable. Over time, this change will reframe our minds, and we develop a more optimistic outlook on life's hurdles.

Learning to replace catastrophic thinking with more realistic and helpful thoughts can lead to greater happiness and personal growth. Facing fears instead of running away from them creates opportunities to learn from mistakes, connect with others, and enjoy life. Every challenge holds a lesson, and allowing ourselves to accept these challenges instead of avoiding them opens doors to new experiences. Building this mindset takes time, but the benefits are profound and lasting.

Once we notice when we are connected to the urge to catastrophize, we can slowly begin working on healthier thought patterns, even if it takes effort.

### All-Or-Nothing Thinking

On the other hand, all-or-nothing thinking, also known as black-and-white thinking, tends to oversimplify our experiences. It forces us to categorize everything into extremes. For instance, if you are working on a project and it does not turn out exactly as you had hoped, you might consider the entire project a failure rather than recognizing the aspects that went well. These thought patterns prevent us from seeing the shades of gray that exist in the world.

All-or-nothing thinking can show up in many parts of our lives. Think about what would happen to a student who struggles with this mindset. If they don't get an A on an exam, they might throw their hands up in defeat and believe they will never succeed in school. They may ignore their past achievements or the fact that most students face challenges. This approach can also creep into our relationships. For instance, if a friend forgets a birthday, it might feel like the friendship is over. Instead of recognizing that people make mistakes, it can lead to hurt feelings and unnecessary distance.

This way of thinking usually stems from early experiences or learned behavior. Perhaps a child grows up in an environment where anything less than perfection is criticized. They learn to view life as a series of successes or failures, with no middle ground. This can create pressure and, ultimately, anxiety. The constant need to excel can consume our thoughts, making us feel inadequate when we inevitably fall short. It raises the question: How many moments do we miss because we are so focused on being perfect?

In everyday conversations, you might hear someone say, "If I can't be the best, then I don't want to try." This attitude can also surface in workplaces. Employees may avoid taking on new tasks if they fear they won't execute them flawlessly. This fear can stifle creativity and growth, not only for them but for the entire team. It makes you wonder how many brilliant ideas have been left on the table due to this fear of not achieving an ideal outcome.

What's even more deadly is that this cognitive distortion can also affect our self-worth. When someone thinks, "I am either a success or a complete failure," they risk defining themselves by their mistakes rather than their efforts. Finding a way to challenge this mindset is important. Instead of saying, "I failed at that," a better perspective might be, "I learned something from that experience." Changing the language we use about ourselves and our experiences can lead to a more balanced view. It encourages growth and acceptance. It's not always easy, but the rewards can be life-changing.

## IMPACT ON SELF-DOUBT AND DECISION-MAKING

The way we think can have a significant impact on self-doubt and our ability to make decisions. Just like what we see when we engage in catastrophizing, that's when we often focus on all the ways things might go wrong instead of seeing the potential for success that exists. We saw how this kind of thinking can create a paralyzing effect, leaving us stuck in a cycle of indecision. At times, we might avoid making choices altogether because we are fixated on the worst-case scenarios. All-or-nothing thinking does not allow for the nuances that life presents. When we set rigid expectations, we open ourselves up to disappointment. If we believe that anything less than perfection means we have failed, the pressure can feel overwhelming, and this automatically stifles our growth and creativity. Below are 21 tips for beating self-doubt whenever you see it creep in:

1.  Challenge negative thoughts. When a doubt creeps in, take a moment to question it. Ask yourself if it's true or if there's evidence against it.
2.  Identify your strengths. Write down things you're good at and past successes. Remind yourself of these when self-doubt arises.
3.  Practice self-compassion. Treat yourself with the same kindness you would show a friend. Understand that everyone struggles with self-doubt at times.
4.  Set realistic goals. Break tasks into smaller, manageable steps. Celebrate small victories along the way.
5.  Visualize success. Picture yourself succeeding in your goals. Create a mental image of how that success feels.
6.  Talk it out. Share your feelings of self-doubt with a trusted friend or mentor. Speaking about it can help normalize your feelings and provide support.
7.  Avoid comparisons. Focus on your own journey instead of comparing yourself to others. Everyone's path is unique and different.
8.  Journaling helps. Write down your thoughts and feelings. This can bring clarity to your mind and help you process your emotions.
9.  Practice mindfulness. Engage in meditation or deep breathing exercises to cultivate present-moment awareness. This can reduce anxiety about the future.
10. Surround yourself with positivity. Spend time with people who uplift you and inspire you to overcome doubts.
11. Accept that mistakes happen. Understand that making mistakes is a part of learning. No one is perfect, and errors are opportunities to grow.

12. Limit exposure to negativity. Whether it's social media or overly critical people, reduce the amount of negativity in your life.
13. Recognition of triggers. Identify situations that provoke self-doubt and develop strategies to cope with them.
14. Embrace uncertainty. Understand that it's okay not to have all the answers right away. Life is a journey filled with unknowns.
15. Seek professional help. Consulting with a therapist can provide tools and strategies to handle self-doubt effectively.
16. Create a positive mantra. Develop a phrase or saying that inspires confidence. Repeat it to yourself regularly.
17. Practice gratitude. Focus on the things you appreciate in life. Gratitude can shift your mindset from negativity to positivity.
18. Limit overthinking. Set a time limit for decision-making. Trust yourself to make choices without prolonged rumination.
19. Engage in activities you enjoy. Doing things you're passionate about can boost your mood and confidence.
20. Focus on what you can control. Redirect your energy to aspects of the situation that you have influence over rather than worrying about uncontrollable factors.
21. Be patient with yourself. Recognize that overcoming self-doubt is a process and allows for ups and downs along the way.

## HOW TO NOTICE OUR DISTORTED THOUGHT PATTERNS

Knowing our cognitive distortions helps us gain control over our minds and thoughts. Several exercises can be particularly useful for identifying these negative thought patterns. Let's have a look at some of them:

- **Thought journaling:** You can start to keep a thought journal. Whenever you notice a negative thought, write it down, along with what type of distortion it represents. For example, if you wrote down, "I always mess things up," you might label it as all-or-nothing thinking. Over time, this practice can help you become more aware of repeating patterns in your thinking.
- **Cognitive restructuring:** We can do this exercise by questioning each distorted thought we have. Before believing or taking those thoughts as fact, take a moment to ask yourself something like this: *Is there evidence to support this thought?* or *What is a more balanced way to view this situation?* When you do this, it becomes a lot easier to see where your thoughts might be ungrounded or just fear-induced fictional thoughts.
- **Mindfulness:** Engaging in mindfulness can help us counteract cognitive distortions because it centers us in the present moment, which can reduce the power of negative thoughts over us. For instance, when you find yourself spiraling into catastrophic thinking, you can take a moment to focus on your breath. By bringing your awareness to your breath, you can remind yourself that not every thought you have reflects reality. Strengthening the habit of gratitude can help balance out the negative. When we write down things we appreciate each day, we can combat the natural negativity bias and restore a more balanced perspective. Mindfulness also helps us achieve greater depths of self-awareness. We can begin to identify the distorted thoughts within ourselves and understand where they come from. As we increase our awareness, we can learn to pause before reacting to these thoughts. This pause is crucial because it provides a moment to choose a more balanced response rather than simply responding with fear and negativity.

## CHALLENGE YOUR UNHELPFUL BELIEFS

Are you ready to equip yourself with tools to evaluate and reframe negative thoughts? Understanding Misdirected Thinking

Misdirected thinking can lead us to paths that are not productive. As shared earlier, it can even harm our self-worth and hinder our progress. To fight against this, it's important to ask ourselves critical questions that challenge our negative beliefs. For example, we might ask, "What evidence is there to support this thought?" or "Is this thought based on facts or just emotions?" These questions serve as a mental check. As we question our thoughts, we can find out if they are based on reality or if they are distorted by our fears and anxieties. This practice helps us to take a step back and assess our inner dialogue more objectively.

Negative beliefs often stem from past experiences or messages we've received from others. They can become so ingrained that they feel like truths. Take time to understand the origins of these thoughts. When we understand where they come from, we can separate them from our current reality. For instance, if someone told us we were not good enough, that belief might linger long after the conversation. Acknowledging that this was someone else's opinion can help us distance ourselves from it and see it for what it is—a misdirected thought.

An effective strategy is to engage in *thought-stopping techniques.* Whenever we notice a negative thought creeping in, we can mentally shout, "Stop!" This helps disrupt the cycle of negativity. After pausing, we can replace that thought with a more constructive one. This technique is a powerful way to break free from the hold that unhelpful beliefs have over us. Over time, these interruptions can help reduce the frequency of negative thinking, paving the way for a healthier mindset.

Tracking our thoughts through journaling can also be beneficial in this process. Writing down negative beliefs and countering them with evidence can help us visualize the difference. This exercise clarifies our thinking and shows us patterns we might not have noticed before. Over time, it becomes easier to identify recurring negative thoughts and challenge them effectively. The act of writing can also serve as a release, allowing us to express emotions that we might otherwise hold inside.

Patience with ourselves remains key throughout this process. Change takes time, and it's natural to slip back into old habits. Instead of judging ourselves for these moments, we can practice self-compassion. Everyone has challenging days, so we need to be kinder to ourselves. We can remind ourselves that each step toward reframing our thoughts is a step in the right direction, no matter how small.

Challenging unhelpful beliefs requires effort, but the reward is worth it. As we build resilience and change our internal dialogue, we open doors to new possibilities. Just remembering that we have control over our thoughts can be empowering. With practice, we can cultivate a mindset that supports our growth and happiness, leading us to a more fulfilling life. The phrases below can help you challenge any negative beliefs that may resurface:

- What evidence contradicts this thought?
- What would I tell a friend in a similar situation?
- Are there alternative explanations for this situation?
- How is this thought serving me, and is there a better way to think?
- What would happen if I let go of this belief?
- How would the person I want to be think or act in this situation?
- What positive outcomes can arise from this situation?

- What have I learned from past experiences that can help now?
- Can I accept that I don't have to be perfect?
- How can I reframe this thought to make it more constructive?

### Dealing With Irrational Fears

When facing irrational fears, we can use strategies to redirect our thinking. We can start to deal with fear by breaking it down into smaller, manageable parts. For instance, if public speaking makes you anxious, start by identifying which specific part worries you the most. Are you scared of forgetting what to say? Or maybe you fear being judged by others? Once you pinpoint the source of your fear, you can address each part separately.

When you focus on what you can control, like preparing your speech or practicing in front of a mirror, you can slowly start changing those overwhelming feelings into a more logical approach. This shift in perspective allows you to take constructive steps instead of feeling paralyzed by fear. It helps to think of this process as building a bridge from fear to action, where every step taken builds your confidence.

## CHANGE YOUR SELF-DEFEATING STATEMENTS

Next, let's look at how we can change self-defeating thoughts such as *I can't* into more empowering possibilities like *What if I could?* The way we talk to ourselves has a tremendous impact on our motivation. When you notice yourself saying "I can't," pause and reframe that to ask, "What steps can I take to make this possible?" or "How can I overcome this challenge?" This shift opens up new avenues instead of closing the door on potential.

Reframing our internal dialogue can boost our confidence because it encourages us to focus not on our limitations but on the possibilities ahead of us. Each small step we take to change our thoughts helps dissolve our cognitive bias. Instead of getting caught up in negative self-talk, we create a more positive mindset that empowers us to take action.

### Real-Life Examples of Reframing

We can look at real-life examples to see how reframing our thoughts can make a difference. Take Jane, for instance. She once believed she was terrible at math. Rather than accepting this as a true statement, she began asking herself, *What can I do to get better?* and *Where can I find help?* This change in questioning helped Jane to take charge of her learning. She shifted from a mindset of fear to one of curiosity and growth.

Another example is Alex, who thought he couldn't chase his dream job because he lacked the right qualifications. Rather than giving in to this belief, he started thinking, *What skills do I need to learn?* and *Who could guide me along the way?* This thought process led him to seek out training and mentorship, which eventually put him on the path to success.

These stories illustrate how powerful reframing can be. So, never forget to look beyond your immediate constraints, and always dare to envision the potential that lies ahead. Adopting this mindset allows us to become more equipped to handle life's challenges. We also develop a willingness to adapt and grow, thus reducing the impact of toxic positivity that can sometimes ignore real issues.

### Guidelines for Evaluating Negative Thoughts

Setting up guidelines can help us evaluate negative thoughts and decide the best actions to take. To do this, consider following the steps below:

1. Create clear, actionable steps to structure your thinking. Start by identifying the negative thought you want to address and write it down.
2. Evaluate this thought using the critical questions: Is it based on facts, or is it influenced by irrational beliefs? If the thought seems to come from a negative place, take a moment to reframe it.
3. Write down alternative views or questions that lead to positive actions.
4. Track any changes you notice in your feelings or perspectives as you follow these steps.

This practice helps in the present and prepares you for future moments when you might encounter similar thought patterns. As you make this reflective practice a habit, you become better at managing unhelpful thoughts over time, leading to progressive personal growth.

## BUILDING A FRAMEWORK FOR RATIONAL THINKING

Rational thinking is fundamentally about clarity and objectivity. This approach requires stepping back from our emotions and focusing on the facts. Critical inquiry encourages questioning assumptions and seeking evidence before drawing conclusions. It does not involve ignoring emotions but using them as data to support our decisions without letting them dictate them.

### *Differentiating Fact From Fiction*

A key aspect of rational thinking is the ability to distinguish between fact and fiction. In today's world, where information is abundant, distinguishing between accurate information and misinformation can sometimes be challenging. Misinformation can often present itself as truth. To fight against this, try to exercise a mindset of skepticism—the kind that is healthy rather than cynical. As shared earlier, this means asking questions like, "What evidence supports this claim?" or "Are there other explanations?" Developing this habit builds a reliable framework for evaluating information objectively.

### Benefits of Fact-Based Analysis

Exercising fact-based analysis in both personal and professional situations can lead to numerous advantages. First, it reduces the chances of making decisions that are based on faulty assumptions or emotional responses. Decisions made using concrete data and verified information are more likely to result in positive outcomes. In a workplace setting, this might mean utilizing performance metrics to assess team effectiveness rather than relying solely on instinct. On a personal level, it could mean looking at a situation through all the available facts instead of jumping to conclusions based on first impressions.

A fact-based approach boosts credibility. People are more likely to listen to arguments rooted in reality rather than mere rhetoric. Whether you are negotiating a business deal or discussing plans with friends, using clear, evidence-based reasoning can strengthen your position. It builds trust, as others are reassured by your commitment to seeking the truth and making well-informed decisions.

### Making Rational Thinking a Habit: Using Logic to Counter Emotional Overwhelm

Creating systems and routines that encourage logical analysis can facilitate logical thinking. For example, you might set aside time each week for reflection. During this time, you can identify instances where emotional responses may have taken precedence over reason. Document situations and examine them from an objective standpoint; this can help you trace patterns in your decision-making and make necessary adjustments.

Surround yourself with people who value rational discourse. Engaging with peers who constructively challenge your ideas can help to build an environment that promotes thoughtful debate. Such interactions encourage refining your arguments and considering various perspectives, which, in turn, enhances your analytical skills.

Using logic to counter emotional overwhelm caused by negative thoughts requires us to break down those overwhelming feelings into manageable parts. Always try to identify the specific negative thought causing distress and ask yourself what evidence supports or refutes that thought. For instance, if you believe *you will always fail*, explore past experiences where you succeeded despite challenges. Acknowledging these successes can disrupt the cycle of negativity. Challenging the validity of negative thoughts through logic helps you create a more balanced view of situations.

Developing a structured approach to confront emotions supports this practice. A simple method is the "if-then" strategy. If a negative thought arises, then you can counter it with a logical statement. For example, "If I think I will fail, then I will remember my past achievements." This technique shifts focus from emotional turmoil to rational reassessment. Writing these thoughts down allows for clearer analysis, reinforcing the reminder that thoughts are not facts and can be examined critically.

Discussing your thoughts with someone you trust can provide fresh insights. They can offer alternative perspectives that you might have overlooked. When you verbalize your thoughts, it clarifies your reasoning and exposes any flawed logic. Expressing your ideas to others often leads to constructive feedback, which enhances your ability to think critically about your emotions.

Establishing a routine can solidify logical thinking as a habit. Schedule regular times to assess your feelings and thoughts. Consistency in this practice can change how you respond to negative emotions over time.

Lastly, engaging in activities that promote logical thinking can also be beneficial. Puzzles, games, or even debates can help sharpen analytical skills while providing a necessary distraction from negative emotions. When you challenge yourself intellectually, you enhance your capacity for rational thought, making it easier to counter emotional overwhelm in everyday scenarios.

### Integrating Rational Thinking Into Daily Life

Integrating rational thinking into daily routines can help transform it into a habitual practice rather than an effortful task. You can start by applying these principles to small decisions in everyday life. For instance, you might analyze different options when deciding what to eat for dinner or selecting the best route to drive home. Gradually, this rational mindset will extend to more significant life decisions. Setting physical or digital reminders can also help prompt you to pause and objectively analyze situations. A simple sticky note on your computer screen asking, "Is this based on fact?" can serve as a constant reminder to embrace rationality.

### Learn from Experiences

For rational thinking to become a sustainable practice, celebrating successes while staying open to improvement is key. Reflecting on past decisions that were based on rational analysis reinforces your commitment to this approach. At the same time, analyzing decisions that did not yield the desired outcome is valuable. This reflection offers insightful learning experiences. By investigating what went wrong and why, you can strengthen your rational framework and learn to avoid similar mistakes in the future.

## IMPLEMENTING PRACTICAL EXERCISES

In the pursuit of separating fact from fiction, try to engage with exercises that encourage critical thinking and self-reflection. These activities are designed to solidify your understanding of cognitive distortions and rational thinking by applying these concepts in real-world settings. Let's walk through a structured approach to ensure you can start this practice effectively.

1. First, diving into step-by-step exercises can be immensely helpful. Begin with identifying a specific scenario where you often feel challenged by unhelpful thoughts—perhaps when preparing for a presentation or making important decisions. Write down the automatic thoughts that arise in these situations. Once documented, examine each one critically: Are these thoughts based on evidence? Do they reflect reality? This exercise highlights cognitive distortions and enables you to see patterns in your thinking.

2. Guided practice sessions can be highly effective in reinforcing this identification process. Set aside time weekly to sit quietly and reflect on your thoughts using prompts or questions like *What am I assuming?* or *Is there another way to view this situation?* Structured reflection helps deepen your insight into how certain thought patterns impact your reactions and decisions. Consider using meditation techniques to calm your mind before these sessions, allowing you to be more clear and focused during your reflection.

3. Remember to track your progress through regular self-assessment as well. Establish a routine check-in with yourself to evaluate how far you've come in diminishing distorted thoughts and embracing rational thinking. Use simple rating scales to assess areas like emotional response, decision-making confidence, and reaction flexibility. This self-awareness measures growth and highlights areas needing further work, ensuring continuous improvement.

Overcoming cognitive distortions and sharpening rational thinking are key steps toward reducing self-doubt, countering toxic positivity, and alleviating the fear of failure. Each step forward better equips you to face life's uncertainties with a balanced perspective.

The skills you develop through these practices extend beyond personal growth; they influence how you interact with and interpret the world around you—continuously assessing and adjusting your mental frameworks grounds you with a mindset that values truth and objectivity, setting a foundation for success across all facets of life.

## SUMMARY

Indeed, our minds can play tricks on us with cognitive distortions. However, the beauty of life is that each day, we get a chance to reset and evolve in the way we see things. Being intentional about applying all the helpful strategies discussed in this chapter can help us effectively reprogram our minds for success. Now is the time to no longer be a prisoner of your mind. Our biggest enemy is always the mean inner critic we all battle with. So, to help us address that internal foe, let's hop into the next chapter whenever you're ready.

# STEP 3: REFRAME YOUR INNER CRITIC

An inner critic is that voice in our minds that constantly judges our actions and decisions. It thrives on our fears and doubts, often reminding us of past failures or pointing out what we still need to improve. This critic often convinces us that we're not good enough, making it challenging to take risks or pursue new opportunities. It affects our success by holding us back from pursuing our goals, stunting our growth, and impacting our confidence. Have you ever hesitated to share your ideas because of the harsh whispers in your head? Perhaps that inner critic is just trying to protect us from failure, but in the process, it also limits our potential, which is why we have to change how we respond to it.

Reframing this inner voice requires us to understand the harm it can cause. Instead of viewing the inner critic as an enemy, we can consider it a safety net that sometimes gets overly exaggerated. It tends to misinterpret challenges as threats. When you hear that critical voice, you can take a moment to ask yourself: *Is it really being helpful? Or is it sabotaging my progress?* This kind of self-reflection can shift our perspective from blame to understanding, and with it, we can begin to reshape the dialogue within our minds.

Changing our inner critic into an ally requires skill, and that's what this chapter will guide us to master. Knowing the roots and intentions behind our critical inner voice is like unlocking a door to a room we've always been curious about but never dared to enter. This voice, often shaped by past experiences and societal norms, is not an arbitrary construction of our minds. It's a reflection of where we come from, what we've lived through, and how we've perceived ourselves in society's mirror.

Think back to a time when someone you respected perhaps gave you harsh feedback. Maybe it was a teacher who pointed out a flaw in your approach or a family member who had certain expectations. These moments leave their mark. Over time, they accumulate and morph into that inner critic you may often struggle to silence. Societal norms also play a significant role. The constant demands for perfection, success, and fitting into predefined roles can amplify this critical voice, making us question our worth and capabilities.

Our inner critic isn't always there to pull us down. Sometimes, it acts as a guardian, trying to shield us from potential failures or disappointments. It might whisper cautionary tales drawn from past mistakes, urging us to think twice before leaping. On the other hand, there are instances where this voice becomes overbearing and damaging, leading to feelings of inadequacy and self-doubt. Distinguishing these instances helps us decide which voice to heed and which to challenge.

Reframing the inner critic means changing how we view the messages it sends. Instead of seeing it solely as a negative force, we can shift our perspective to see it as a source of insight. When we practice reframing, we start to notice patterns within our internal conversations. It becomes clear that the inner critic often repeats familiar narratives. As we learn to manage our inner landscapes with empathy and kindness, we equip ourselves to face external chal-lenges with greater strength. Each encounter with this voice becomes an opportunity for deeper understanding and personal growth, allowing us to embrace life's uncertainties with open hearts. Now, let's move forward to unpack some key strategies we can use to actively reframe our inner critic.

## SHIFT FROM CRITICISM TO CONSTRUCTIVE FEEDBACK

Many of us experience an inner critic that often highlights our flaws instead of our strengths. This internal dialogue can be overwhelm-ing, but we can learn to use it as a guide instead of a burden by changing our perception of it. One helpful technique to consider is *interpreting self-criticism as constructive advice.* For instance, if your inner voice claims you are not good enough at a task, take a moment to ask yourself what specific steps you could take to improve in that area. Instead of feeling defeated by this criticism, you turn it into a motivation for positive action.

### *Visualization Exercises*

Visualization exercises can play a vital role in changing the tone of your inner voice. Visualize your inner critic speaking to you in a kinder and more supportive way. Imagine what they might say if they were acting as a coach instead of a detractor. Envision your inner critic encouraging you after a setback, offering suggestions for improvement, or congratulating you on your achievements. Regu-larly practicing this kind of visualization can help your mind develop a more positive and nurturing inner dialogue. You begin to rewrite the script of how your mind communicates with you, thus creating a healthier relationship with yourself.

### Success Stories of Transformation

Let's consider some success stories that illustrate how people have reshaped their self-dialogue for the better. Take Malia, for example. She is a young professional who constantly deals with an unyielding inner critic. After attending a workshop focused on self-compassion, Malia learned to pause when she experienced negative self-talk. She began asking herself, *What would I say to a friend in this situation?* When she applied this approach, Malia found herself feeling increasingly confident and less anxious about future challenges. Her experience shows the incredible power of perspective and empathy in altering self-perception.

Now, let's consider Tom's story. As a writer, Tom faced intense self-doubt every time he attempted to create. To confront this issue, he began journaling to uncover the nature of his inner criticisms. This practice allowed him to identify recurring themes and understand that many of his fears were rooted in past failures. With this understanding, Tom reframed his inner dialogue to focus more on learning and growth. Each stumble became an opportunity for improvement rather than a reason for self-criticism.

These examples show us that reframing feedback can significantly impact personal growth. When we learn to transform criticism into constructive advice, we gain power. Change becomes feasible because we break free from the confines of negative thinking. Empowerment arises from viewing challenges not as roadblocks but as learning opportunities that help us evolve.

### Break Down Criticism

A practical tip that can make this transformation easier is to break down criticisms into smaller, more manageable parts. For example, if your inner critic says, "You're not good at public speaking," take a close look at that statement. Identify what specific aspects of your public speaking could be improved. Is it your pace, clarity, or body language? Once you clarify these areas, set small, achievable goals for yourself to tackle each one at a time. This approach not only promotes improvement but also boosts your sense of accomplishment and confidence.

### Structured Techniques for Transformation

Having structured techniques can help us change self-criticism into actionable guidance. Start by writing down the critical things your inner voice says. Then, reflect on the statements and ask yourself, *Is there any truth to this? Can I turn this criticism into a question that encourages action?* For example, change a statement like "I'm terrible at this" into a question such as "How can I become better at this?" This simple shift changes your mindset from one of defeat to one focused on curiosity and problem-solving

## REPLACE NEGATIVE MESSAGES FROM YOUR INNER CRITIC WITH POSITIVE, EMPOWERING AFFIRMATIONS

Replacing negative messages from our inner critic with positive affirmations can change the way we view ourselves and our capabilities. Switching from thoughts that belittle our efforts and achievements to uplifting phrases changes our mindset. This shift helps us build confidence and push through challenges. Hence, take a moment to think about and list any harmful messages that linger in your mind and write them down. Once done, you can actively replace them with affirmations that empower you instead. This practice can dissolve our self-doubt and open doors to success we once thought were closed.

Negative self-talk often manifests in various forms, such as feelings of unworthiness or fear of failure. Each negative assertion represents a barrier keeping us from reaching our full potential. To break down these barriers, we can create a list of common negative messages along with positive affirmations to counter them. Consistently using these affirmations reinforces our belief in ourselves and keeps the inner critic in check.

- "I am not good enough." → "I am capable and deserving of success."
- "I always mess things up." → "I learn and grow from my experiences."
- "Nobody cares what I think." → "My thoughts and opinions are valuable."
- "I will never achieve my goals." → "Every step I take brings me closer to my goals."
- "I am a failure." → "I embrace my journey and learn from my mistakes."
- "People will laugh at me." → "I share my truth, and it resonates with others."
- "I am not as talented as others." → "My unique skills and talents are my strengths."
- "I shouldn't even try." → "Trying is part of the journey, and I can handle it."
- "I am not worthy of love." → "I am worthy of love and respect."
- "I am always anxious." → "I am learning to manage my emotions with grace."
- "I can't handle pressure." → "I rise to challenges with confidence."
- "I am invisible." → "I shine brightly and am seen by those who matter."
- "I don't deserve happiness." → "I actively seek and embrace happiness."
- "I am too old to start over." → "It's never too late to pursue my passions."
- "I can't make decisions." → "I trust my intuition and make choices confidently."

Using these affirmations allows us to counteract negative self-talk. Integrating them into daily routines can create a habit that reinforces positivity. Each repetition boosts our self-esteem and reinforces our conviction that we indeed have the power to change our mindset and our lives.

Daily affirmations can be incorporated into morning rituals or moments of doubt throughout the day. This consistency is key; the more we tell ourselves these positive truths, the more we internalize them. Over time, the volume of our inner critic diminishes as we confront its messages with unwavering positivity.

In moments of self-doubt, we can turn to our list of affirmations for quick inspiration. They become tools readily available to combat negative thoughts during life's challenges. When we face setbacks, instead of succumbing to discouraging thoughts, we can lean into our affirmations to remind ourselves of our capabilities.

Adopting this mindset not only benefits us individually but can also have a positive impact on our interactions with others. When we exude confidence and self-assurance, it encourages those around us to embrace their strengths and challenge their critics, too. Our energy becomes contagious, igniting a spark of positivity in our friendships, family, and workplaces.

We witness a massive shift in our lives as we replace negative messages with empowering affirmations. Our goals become more tangible as we recognize our capabilities. The light that once seemed dim starts to shine brighter, illuminating paths once hidden by doubts. Our outlook transforms from hesitance to enthusiasm, signaling a chapter of growth and success.

Once you start working on changing your inner monologue, consider tracking your progress. You can keep a journal to jot down reflections on how affirmations impact your day-to-day experiences. This practice serves as a reminder of your growth and the power of shifting your inner dialogue. The change takes time, but with every positive affirmation and every moment we challenge our inner critic, we step closer to becoming the best version of ourselves.

## MAINTAINING A SUPPORTIVE MENTAL DIALOGUE

We saw how developing and maintaining a nurturing and balanced internal conversation can change how we see ourselves and what we believe we can achieve. This change begins with bringing self-compassion and accountability together. Although these two ideas may appear to be opposites, they actually wonderfully complement each other. Think of self-compassion as a gentle voice that helps you feel understood, while accountability is the part of you that keeps you responsible for what you do. Combining these qualities allows you to treat yourself kindly when you experience challenges but still recognize where you can improve and grow.

### Balancing Self-Compassion with Accountability

To balance self-compassion with accountability is quite important. Start by taking note of your feelings without being judgmental. It's perfectly okay to feel disappointed when things do not work out as you had planned. However, refrain from being overly critical of yourself. Instead of saying something harsh like, "I failed again," think about it differently by saying, "This is a chance for me to learn." This shift in perspective is essential. After acknowledging your feelings, it is beneficial to hold yourself accountable by setting realistic goals for improvement. If you notice what went wrong, focus on how you can do better next time instead of just feeling bad about it. Ask questions such as, "What changes can I make?" or "How can I handle this situation differently?" This approach keeps you compassionate toward yourself while also encouraging personal growth.

### *Daily Practices to Nurture a Constructive Mindset*

Integrating daily practices can help solidify a constructive mindset. These practices don't need to be complicated; in fact, keeping them simple often leads to better consistency. A few minutes of mindfulness is a great way to start your day. This practice helps to organize your thoughts and creates a positive start. Take time to reflect on your day at the end of each day; this can be a very powerful practice as it allows you to be more aware of your thought patterns and how they impact your decisions throughout the day. Look back on both your achievements and the aspects that might need improvement. To add more structure, create a checklist of mindful activities to incorporate into your routine. This will help you stay committed to nurturing a positive mindset.

When your internal voice shifts from critical to encouraging, it can positively impact many areas of your life. For example, you may notice that your stress levels decrease because you're less likely to dwell on feelings of failure. Over time, your self-esteem can increase, making you more willing to take risks and explore new opportunities.

## SUMMARY

We saw how our inner critic was formed by our past experiences. That means for us to construct new thought patterns, we have to intentionally expose ourselves to new experiences and messages. Healthy core beliefs and positive and empowering thoughts we want to live by can be engraved in our minds and hearts through practice. When negative thoughts pop up, instead of just trying to suppress them, we can choose to see if we can derive any constructive feedback from those thoughts. This change creates a more empowering perspective, where self-criticism becomes constructive advice, allowing you to focus on personal improvement rather than getting bogged down by negativity.

Now that we've spoken about actively changing our paradigm through reframing negative thoughts, let's hop into the next chapter to unpack more on how we can handle worry. Worry can drain so much of our mental and emotional energy; that's why it's essential to know how to deal with it successfully so it won't keep you trapped in cycles of fear and self-doubt anymore. Are you ready to free your mind and no longer be a victim of chronic worry? I believe you are!

# STEP 4: TURN WORRY INTO ACTION

Doesn't worry remind you of an annoying mosquito that shows up in your room and makes noise all night long when all you want is to simply rest? Funny, but it's true. It drains so much of our energy when it takes the reigns in our minds. It can take many forms—concern about a job interview, anxiety over family matters, or even fretting about what to make for dinner on a busy weeknight. It can stick around for days or weeks or even linger like that weird smell you can't identify. But why does it seem like we get stuck in this worry loop? Is there a manual we missed out on that says worrying is the right way to handle life's curveballs?

Let's face it: Waddling around with worry just drains the life out of us! Why? Because it saps our joy, diminishes our creativity, and sometimes, we forget to breathe! Instead of enjoying the present moment, we end up locked in a mental wrestling match that's not even entertaining. Worry takes what could be relaxing moments and turns them into exhausting patterns for your brain. The dripping faucet of thoughts just keeps running and running. *Did I send that email? What if I trip on stage? Is there broccoli in my teeth?* The mind can turn a simple situation into a full-blown tragedy—Oscar-worthy performances included!

Now, let's give a round of applause to our overactive imaginations! If we could harness that energy for good instead of spinning scenarios that lead to panic, we might just become superheroes. Ever find yourself daydreaming—scratch that, day-dreading—about the future? You know, picturing yourself forgetting your lines in a play, or worse, showing up to the party in your pajamas? Those thoughts can mushroom into something explosive. But what if we took those moments of "What if?" and flipped them? Instead of saying, "What if I embarrass myself?" how about, "What if I rock it and get a standing ovation?" Easier said than done, right?! That's why this chapter will help us put on our invisible cheerleader outfits and think of how we can turn those worries back into action!

## WHAT IS ACTIONABLE WORRY?

We can't always dodge every worry, but we can respond to it. Some concerns, of course, are worth paying attention to. They act like signposts telling us there's work to be done or changes to be made. So, let's chat about the power of *actionable worry*. Maybe you're worried about not having enough savings. Instead of letting that keep you awake at night, why not draw up a budget or think of ways to cut expenses? You can turn it into a productive worry fiesta! You can invite your worries to motivate you, not demoralize you. "Oh, I'm worried I can't run that marathon? Well, guess who just signed up for a training program?" That's right—when the worries come, the action can follow right behind.

Think of worries as little nudges from the universe or some cosmic personal trainers! You know they're nudging you, saying, "Hey, focus on this. Let's turn you into a better version of yourself." Sure, it's no walk in the park, but the longer we sit and stew on those worries without turning them into action, the heavier they can become. It's like carrying around a backpack full of rocks. So, let's lighten that load! Write down what's bothering you, brainstorm possible responses, recruit your trusty sidekick (hello, whoever's nearest), and get moving. Worry may want to crash the party, but you can definitely be the one in charge of the playlist!

As we swap out anxiety for action, we acknowledge those feelings. It's perfectly okay to fret sometimes—it's a natural human response! But that doesn't mean you have to stay glued to your couch in worry-ville. Ask yourself: *What's the worst that could happen?* Spoiler alert: Sometimes, it's not as bad as we think. In fact, most of the time, it's not even close. What really matters is recognizing when those thoughts serve a purpose versus when they just hijack your brain.

What if you start a gratitude jar for those days when worry decides to mind its own business? Write down what you're grateful for or what you've achieved, no matter how tiny. Get in the habit of switching gears, and soon, it all becomes second nature. Grab that worry, look it in the face, and say, "Thanks for your input, but I'm far too busy being awesome!" And just like that, you've transformed unproductive spirals into uplifting actions. Pretty neat, right? This foundation sets the stage for transforming worries into clear, action-able steps, empowering you to confidently move forward.

## HOW TO DISTINGUISH BETWEEN PRODUCTIVE AND UNPRODUCTIVE WORRIES

Knowing how to turn worry into action is a valuable skill. This skill can improve your life in many ways. A good starting point is to know which worries you can actually do something about and which ones drain your energy. Differentiating between these two categories is key.

When worry lingers in your mind, it's a good idea to take a moment to think about its nature. Ask yourself if this worry can lead to a solution or if it's just taking up space in your mind. Worries that can be acted upon often point to areas for change in your life. On the other hand, worries that have no clear steps to take are usually beyond your control. These concerns can mentally exhaust you without offering any benefits (AH Admin, 2022).

### Use Lists to Manage Worries

One way to deal with nagging worries is to use lists. Lists can break down overwhelming thoughts into manageable pieces. That means get your pen and paper (or your digital notebook) ready and start writing down your worries. List as many as you can think of. Notice the relief you start feeling after emptying those worries out. This practice helps you gain a clearer perspective. When you make a list of each worry, beside each one, note whether it is something you can act on. This method not only helps you understand your concerns better but also makes it easier to decide on the next steps.

Seeing your worries on paper can help you prioritize what truly needs attention. If a worry is actionable, you can create a plan for addressing it. If it's not, being aware of it can free up your mental space, meaning this simple act of listing starts to bring you clarity and focus, making challenges feel less daunting.

### Cognitive Exercises for Reframing Thoughts

In addition to lists, cognitive exercises can help you manage any lingering worrying thoughts. These exercises assist in challenging and reframing negative beliefs. One simple but effective exercise is to take a bothersome thought and repeatedly ask, "Is this thought true?" Often, our minds run wild with what-if scenarios that are unlikely to happen. This is why noticing and questioning these thoughts can greatly reduce your stress.

Pair this exercise with writing down potential solutions to your worries. When you write out possible actions, you will find that your worries seem more manageable, making this practice a helpful way to change negative thoughts into tangible steps you can take.

### Mind Mapping to Visualize Worries

Mind mapping is a cool visual way to effectively handle worries. This method allows you to visualize and organize your worries. To practice mind mapping, start with your main concern in the center of a page. Then, branch out into related thoughts and possible actions. This visual representation helps clarify your thoughts and highlights priorities and connections that may not be immediately obvious.

The act of seeing everything mapped out can change chaos into clear pathways for action. Engaging in this creative process will likely spark new ideas and solutions you may not have considered before.

### Set a Regular Time for Worry Management

Consider scheduling regular times for these activities. Practicing consistently enhances your ability to deal with worries effectively. This approach empowers you to actively work through your thoughts rather than allowing them to overwhelm you throughout the day. Establishing a routine around these exercises forms a strong habit of turning worry into action. As you may already know, worry doesn't like being ignored; that's why assuring yourself that you will attend to those worries at a designated time can help you calm down and be able to focus on other things.

Knowing that you have dedicated time for this practice makes it easier to confront your worries. This routine can also help you stay focused and grounded in the process, making it feel more manageable.

Assess the control you have over your worries. This means regularly asking if a worry is something you can control. When a concern arises, pause to consider, "Is there anything I can do about this right now?" If the answer is yes, think about what steps you can take immediately or plan to take later. If the answer is no, practice letting it go.

Shifting your focus from worries that have no immediate solution to actionable tasks enhances your mental well-being and productivity. It encourages a healthier mindset and allows you to focus on what truly matters.

Recognizing worries to address doesn't mean you should ignore all your worries. Instead, learn to discern which ones are worth your attention. With practice, you can direct your energy toward issues you can genuinely impact. This skill can shift how you approach challenges in your life, leading to a more empowered mindset.

## DEVELOPING A PRE-MORTEM STRATEGY

Life often throws unexpected challenges our way, and it can be tempting to let worry take over. When we focus too much on what might go wrong, we can become paralyzed by fear. However, taking a moment to prepare for these challenges can turn our anxiety into constructive action. For example, think about carrying an umbrella on a day when there's only a slight chance of rain. You do it so you're ready if it rains, and if it doesn't rain, you feel relieved. Planning for the worst-case scenario works in the same way.

### *The Importance of Planning*

To effectively address concerns, it is helpful to follow structured steps. These steps can help us analyze projects or goals from a preemptive angle rather than a reactive one. One useful method is conducting a *pre-mortem analysis*. This means you picture a future where your project has failed completely. This exercise isn't about being negative; it's a way to prepare yourself for any potential setbacks. To do that, start by asking why things have gone wrong in this imagined scenario. What were the factors that led to this failure? By listing out potential problems, you gain clarity on what to watch for and how to address them before they become a real issue.

### Involve Others in the Process

A vital part of this planning approach will require us to engage our team or peers in the pre-mortem analysis. It's important to encourage open conversations where everyone can share their thoughts on possible failures. Such collaborative efforts not only bring in a variety of perspectives but also stimulate creative problem-solving. When team members participate in identifying risks, it strengthens the sense of unity and shared responsibility in facing those challenges.

### Real-World Examples of Success

Real-life examples can illustrate how effective pre-mortem thinking can be. Successful leaders often turn potential disasters into opportunities for growth. Jeff Bezos, the founder of Amazon, is a prominent figure who practiced this. He was known for analyzing risks and developing preventive strategies right from the start. Instead of viewing setbacks as failures, he embraced the idea of "failing forward." This approach allowed Amazon to navigate numerous hardships on its way to becoming a major player in the e-commerce market.

### Learn From Personal Experience

Reflecting on our own experiences can also shed light on the benefits of anticipating challenges. Think back to a situation where you prepared for potential roadblocks. For instance, you may have had an important work presentation and were concerned about possible technical issues. To prepare, you saved your files in several formats and practiced your presentation offline. This way, even if something went wrong, you were still ready to deliver your message. Such preparation boosts your confidence and improves your ability to adapt to unforeseen circumstances.

### Empowerment Through Preparation

While it might feel overwhelming to think about worst-case scenarios, this mindset can actually empower us to take control of our situations. When you choose to be proactive rather than reactive, you don't let potential issues dictate your actions. Instead, you circumvent around them, preparing for the "what ifs." This preparation builds a sense of purpose and allows you to act decisively, helping to reduce feelings of anxiety related to uncertainty.

### Balancing Preparation With Optimism

It is essential to strike the right balance between preparing for challenges and maintaining a positive outlook. Focusing too much on what could go wrong can overshadow the excitement of what could go right. While it is wise to prepare for difficulties, it is just as pivotal to let that not diminish our enthusiasm for success. Combining caution with an optimistic view creates a realistic and motivating strategy as we learn to expect and navigate both the ups and downs that life presents.

It is important to approach any project or goal with a clear mind. Prepare by creating a detailed action plan that outlines the steps needed to achieve your objectives. This plan should include potential obstacles you might encounter along the way and strategies to overcome them. By thinking ahead and mapping out your course of action, you will set yourself up for greater success.

### Develop a Risk Mitigation Plan

As you refine your plans, consider developing a risk mitigation plan that outlines specific actions you can take to address the potential issues you identified during your pre-mortem analysis. This might include setting up contingency plans for critical aspects of your project. For instance, if you are working on a project with a tight deadline, create strategies to ensure you stay on track even if one element goes awry. Identifying resources, whether they be additional team members, tools, or processes, can enhance your readiness for any unforeseen setbacks.

### Regularly Review and Update Plans

Once you've created your plans, remember that they should not be static. Review and update them regularly based on new experiences and information. As you move forward, make it a habit to reflect on what has worked and what hasn't. Adaptability is key in any project, and being willing to adjust your approach will help you navigate uncertainty with greater ease.

Finally, nurture a growth mindset as you tackle challenges. Realize that every setback offers an opportunity to learn and grow. Instead of fearing failure, view it as a valuable part of the journey. This mindset helps you remain resilient and motivated, even when things don't go as planned. Focusing on continuous improvement helps you pave the way for future success, turning potential worries into opportunities for development.

## BUILD MOMENTUM WITH SMALL WINS

Turning worry into action begins with understanding how to transform daunting tasks into manageable steps. A common barrier many face when dealing with overwhelming challenges is analysis paralysis, where overthinking stalls any progress. The key here? Break down those large, intimidating tasks into smaller, bite-sized pieces —micro-goals that act like stepping stones rather than hurdles.

Imagine you're starting a major project, like writing a book or launching a business. The sheer magnitude of the task can paralyze you, making it difficult to start. When you set micro-goals, you reduce the risk of getting bogged down by too much information at once. For instance, if your goal is to write a book, start by setting a timeline for brainstorming ideas in one week. Once that's done, move on to outlining a chapter a week. These micro-goals are designed to build momentum and keep you moving forward without feeling overwhelmed.

Each time you reach a milestone, no matter how small, take a moment to acknowledge it. This practice isn't just a pat on the back. It's a big part of reinforcing positive behavior and encouraging further progress. Achieving even minor goals can significantly boost your self-assurance, making the daunting journey ahead appear less intimidating.

Think about how fulfilling it is to check off items from a to-do list. Each checked item is evidence of what you're capable of achieving. This same principle applies to larger life goals. Every small win strengthens your belief in yourself and proves that you're on the right path. Confidence grows incrementally, just like the success itself.

Reflecting on stories of people or teams who embraced incremental progress can be incredibly inspiring. Take, for example, the story of a startup team that felt stuck in a rut, overwhelmed by a seemingly insurmountable project deadline. They decided to divide their workload into daily objectives, assigning specific targets to each team member. As they began ticking off these smaller tasks, their collective confidence surged, driving them to exceed their expectations. The initial baby steps morphed into giant leaps, leading to successful project completion and renewed team spirit.

Then there's the personal tale of an athlete recovering from injury who was initially unable to resume their full training regimen. Instead of focusing on the end goal of returning to competition, they set daily fitness objectives—simple tasks such as walking a little further each day or performing gentle stretches. With each minor triumph, their motivation soared, and their recovery accelerated. These anecdotes show that transforming ambition into actionable steps is fundamental to overcoming obstacles and achieving significant change.

Finally, adopting this approach helps grow a mindset that sees challenges not as threats but as opportunities for growth. When faced with worries, remind yourself that they can be leveraged to initiate positive action. When you deconstruct tasks, boost your self-assurance through small wins, and regularly celebrate progress, you gradually turn the tide of negativity into a wave of constructive energy. In doing so, you empower yourself to push boundaries and redefine what's possible, ultimately unleashing your full potential.

## SUMMARY

Turning worries into actionable steps can truly transform our daily lives. By identifying which concerns are within our control and separating them from those that aren't, we free up mental space for productive thinking. Preparing for uncertainties with tools like premortem analysis helps us manage life's unpredictability. It's like having a backup plan ready to smooth out potential bumps along the way. Remember that breaking daunting tasks into micro-goals keeps progress moving without feeling stuck. Even if the mountain seems high, each small victory builds confidence and momentum. Embracing this mindset means seeing worries not just as obstacles but as opportunities to grow stronger and more resilient. In doing so, we empower ourselves to turn thoughts into tangible success, inching closer to unlocking our full potential.

Gradually, as you incorporate these habits, you'll likely notice a shift not only in how you handle worry but also in your overall outlook. Challenges become less daunting; anxiety becomes more manageable. Ultimately, changing worry into action is about empowerment. It's about reclaiming control over your thoughts and directing them toward meaningful progress. As you set clear intentions and maintain an empowering mindset, you're not just combating negative thoughts but using them to unleash your full potential. Since we often worry about failure and fear it so much, let's now hop into Chapter 5 to explore how we can liberate ourselves from the fear of failure. See you there!

# STEP 5: LEARN AND GROW
# FROM FAILURE

Learning and growing from failure is a common thread in the fabric of our lives. Yet, despite its ubiquity, have you ever wondered why we often shy away from failure as though it's something to be ashamed of? Perhaps, by looking at it differently, we'd see it as a stepping stone rather than a stumbling block. Could seeing failure as a friend rather than a foe change how we tackle challenges? Where does the fear of failure we all seem to struggle with come from? What do you think?

The fear of failure often sprouts from our inner critic, that little voice in our heads that loves to amplify our self-doubt. Many of us may find ourselves clinging to our comfort zones. It feels safe, even if it gets a tad cramped. This resistance to change can stem from the worry of disappointing ourselves or others, or it could just be our brains craving the familiar thrill of Netflix and snacks over scary, life-altering adventures. But what if we swapped our fear for curiosity? Imagine what would happen. Why not ask ourselves what wild new skills we could discover by failing?

When we encounter setbacks, we might think of them as signs that we should toss in the towel. Yet, every failure is like a quirky plot twist in a sitcom. Instead of getting mad, we could choose to laugh it off and ask, "What's the punchline here?" If we choose to let go of perfectionism, we create an open door to innovation. Imagine if Thomas Edison had given up after the first thousand attempts at the lightbulb. He would've missed out on being a household name and would leave us all stumbling around in the dark, quite literally. By looking at our missteps with humor, we invite a refreshing mindset, one where failing becomes part of the adventure rather than the end of the road.

In this chapter, we will look into redefining our relationship with failure. We're about to explore not only our cultural conditioning around success and failure but also specific strategies and exercises that can help us learn from past experiences. As we analyze these themes together, we're preparing to appreciate failure for the unique learning opportunity it presents. Are you ready to look at failure differently and let it guide you toward growth? Let's get started and discover how this shift in perspective can empower and propel us forward in ways we might never have imagined.

## REDEFINING FAILURE

Failure is often seen as something to avoid at all costs. But why do we, as a society, tend to paint failure in such dark colors? Is it because we've been conditioned to equate success with worth and any deviation from that standard as problematic? Let's explore this notion further and perhaps challenge some of our preconceived ideas.

From a young age, many of us are taught to fear failure. Educational systems reward perfect scores and punish mistakes, creating an environment where failure feels like the end rather than a meaningful part of the learning process. Have you ever found yourself paralyzed by the fear of not getting things right the first time? This mindset, deeply ingrained in many cultures, hinders our ability to accept failure as a valuable teacher.

Our perceptions of failure can greatly influence how we approach life's challenges. Why not redefine what failure means to us personally? By doing so, we empower ourselves to pursue goals that initially seem unattainable. Take a moment to think about a situation where you faced disappointment. What would have happened if you viewed that experience merely as a step in your growth rather than a full stop? How would that change your outlook on trying again?

So how do we start this transformation within ourselves? We can begin with introspection and open conversation. Let's engage in a simple exercise:

1. Grab some writing utensils.
2. Write down a past failure—big or small.
3. Reflect on it. What went wrong, and what did you learn from it? Sometimes, simply seeing these moments written out can shift your perspective.
4. Identify a positive outcome that arose from this failure. Perhaps it pushed you to acquire new skills or led you down a more fulfilling path.

The key is to embrace failure as a natural aspect of life—a stepping stone, not a stumbling block. This idea might feel petrifying at first, especially when we're surrounded by messages that emphasize only success. Yet, what if we considered each misstep as evidence of our attempts to strive for something bigger and better? Wouldn't that make the journey all the more rewarding?

The trick is to change how we think about failure. Instead of hyper-focusing on what went wrong, we can ask ourselves what we learned along the way. Remember, even the most successful folks, those who seem to have it all figured out, have plenty of blooper reels tucked away in their closets. They embrace their flops as badges of honor, proving that every epic fail is simply paving the way for a triumphant comeback. So, whip out your diaries and start chronicling your learning journeys because those entries will eventually read like a best-selling novel!

As we rewrite the narrative around failure, we create a rules-free zone where trying new things becomes the new cool. Our lives become a playground, a space for swings and slides and daring experiments. Think of each leap into the unknown, whether it's attempting to dance like nobody's watching or starting that hobby you've put off for years, as opportunities to gain new insights and stories, paving the way for creativity and growth. It's a chance to nurture a mindset that embraces taking risks, learning, and then doing it all over again with even more flair. Every small step we take builds our confidence, slowly encouraging us to tackle larger challenges without the heavy chains of fear. So, are you ready to take the plunge and see what fails end up being the most fun? The adventure awaits!

## EXTRACTING LESSONS FROM SETBACKS

One of the hardest things to endure can be unexpected setbacks. How do you often handle those? A good way to manage unexpected failures or setbacks is to really analyze what went wrong so that we can extract lessons from the experiences. We can start with asking the right questions like *What went wrong? Why did it happen?* These are fundamental queries that guide our exploration. Think of it like peeling an onion—you get layer after layer of understanding. But how do we structure this analysis without getting overwhelmed? We can break it down step by step, much like piecing together a puzzle.

1. Start by listing all the factors involved in the situation—people, processes, and resources.
2. Then, examine each one: Did everything align as planned? Were there unexpected hurdles? By isolating these components, we can see what exactly faltered. Remember, each piece has its story to tell—are you listening closely? But what about the successes? Yes, even in failure, there are gems of success tucked away.
3. Dissect both the good and the bad. This way, you'll start noticing patterns. Are there consistent issues that arise across different experiences? Or perhaps specific strategies always seem to yield positive results. Noticing these trends is where the magic happens—it's where opportunities for improvement and innovation become visible.
4. Note down if you notice a recurring theme in your challenges.

Now, let's talk mindset. Maintaining a positive outlook during this analysis is key. Instead of wallowing in regret, choose to focus on what you can learn. You can utilize the reframing technique we learned earlier and reframe your thoughts: Instead of thinking, *I failed*, consider, *I learned what doesn't work*. This simple shift can lighten the emotional load and redirect your energy toward growth. Do you find yourself stuck in negative thought patterns when analyzing mishaps?

The positive affirmations we spoke about previously also come in handy here, as they often play a role in bolstering our mindset. Remind yourself that every misstep is part of a bigger journey toward personal and professional evolution. Surrounding yourself with supportive voices—be it friends, mentors, or inspirational content—further promotes perseverance. Who do you turn to when you need encouragement in tough times?

Let's put this into practice with some guidelines. First, try exercises that redefine what failure means to you personally.

1. Grab a journal and write about a recent setback.
2. Reflect on what you learned and how you've grown. You might begin to see failure in a new light—not as an end but as a beginning. Have you tried seeing failure through this empowering lens?
3. Next, we perform a thorough failure analysis. Start by creating a timeline of events leading up to the failure. Identify the pivotal moments where things went awry. Then, pull apart each event to understand its impact.
4. Document your findings systematically—it helps in visualizing the whole picture. Afterward, compile your insights. What lessons stand out? Can any be applied to future scenarios? We're not just pondering hypotheticals here—think of a specific event in your life. How would you dissect it using this method?

As you go deeper into your analysis, you will notice that your self-awareness will begin to grow. Perhaps you discover a new skill or realize a strength you never knew you had during a challenging time. Make a note of these positive aspects—they're tools for your future endeavors.

## REINVENTING AFTER FAILURE

How do we regain our footing when life throws us off balance? We all face this question at some point, and the answer lies within each of us. Rebuilding self-confidence after experiencing failure can be the beginning of an exciting new chapter.

Let's talk about self-reflection more. When failure hits, take a moment to sit down and think about what happened. Failure often triggers a whirlwind of emotions that can cloud our judgment. By setting aside time for introspection, we begin to see things more clearly. What were the circumstances that led to this outcome? Did external factors influence the situation, or could different choices have altered the result? This isn't about assigning blame; it's about gaining clarity. Let's learn from the past to build a better future.

Once we've understood where we might have gone wrong, the next step is skill enhancement. How can we turn weaknesses into strengths? Focusing on enhancing existing skills or developing new ones boosts confidence significantly. Consider enrolling in a workshop, taking up a short course, or simply practicing in areas where improvement is needed. Isn't it exciting to think about emerging stronger, with fresh abilities under your belt?

We can't ignore the power of small achievements. They are the stepping stones to regaining confidence. Setting and achieving small, manageable goals builds momentum. Think about celebrating even the tiniest wins in your journey. If your goal is big, break it down. Each mini-success nudges you closer to your ultimate objective, reminding you that progress is being made. How motivating is it to tick tasks off your list and see how far you've come?

Visualization exercises help create a vivid mental image of where we want to be. They can help you start your day each morning filled with purpose, ready to conquer whatever comes your way. Picture yourself succeeding, overcoming obstacles, and savoring the sweet taste of success. Creating such mental blueprints not only reinforces motivation but also brings clarity as we navigate through challenges. Below is a summary of 21 tips you can use to bounce back from failure:

1. Acknowledge your feelings. It's okay to feel upset or disappointed.

2. Take time to reflect on what went wrong. Understanding the root cause is crucial.

3. Set realistic goals. Break them down into smaller, manageable steps.

4. Learn from mistakes. Identify lessons that can propel you forward.

5. Surround yourself with supportive people. Their encouragement can boost your confidence.

6. Practice self-compassion. Treat yourself with kindness and forgive your missteps.

7. Stay positive. Focus on solutions rather than the problems you face.

8. Engage in physical activity. Exercise helps reduce stress and improves mood.

9. Seek help when needed. Talk to friends, family, or professionals.

10. Keep a journal. Writing down your thoughts can provide clarity and insight.

11. Celebrate small victories. Recognizing progress, no matter how tiny, matters.

12. Visualize success. Imagine yourself reaching your goals and the feelings that come with it.

13. Take action. Stay proactive and tackle challenges head-on.

14. Establish a routine. Consistency helps create stability in your life.

15. Embrace new skills. Learning something new can spark motivation and creativity.

16. Get inspired by others. Read stories of people who have overcome challenges.

17. Maintain a growth mindset. Believe that your abilities can improve with effort.

18. Avoid the comparison trap. Everyone's journey is different; focus on your own path.

19. Set boundaries with negativity. Limit exposure to toxic situations or individuals.
20. Seek out new experiences. Trying new things can bring fresh perspectives.
21. Practice gratitude. Focusing on what you're thankful for can shift your mindset.

Changing our perspective can reshape our entire approach to setbacks. What if we saw failure not as a dead-end but as a valuable detour guiding us toward growth? Embracing this mindset enhances resilience. Each challenge becomes less daunting because we understand that stumbling is part of moving forward. Maintaining a positive outlook transforms fear into opportunity—suddenly, failing doesn't seem so scary, does it?

## SUMMARY

This chapter has taught us to reframe our views on failure, seeing it not as an end but as a remarkable lesson. Isn't it refreshing to think about mistakes in such a positive light? We've seen how each stumble can be a building block for bigger dreams. So, next time you face the fear of failing, ask yourself: *What could I learn from this? How could this moment be my stepping stone to something even greater?* So, are you ready to rewrite your narrative around failure? Let's keep questioning, keep learning, and keep moving forward with renewed energy. After all, isn't it exhilarating to know that every setback carries the promise of a comeback? The next chapter will help us strengthen our grit and ability to stay resilient.

# STEP 6: BUILD RESILIENCE THROUGH REALISTIC THINKING

Building resilience means recovering from difficulties and staying positive. But is it a quality we need to beat negativity? Absolutely yes! It helps us find new ways to solve problems, even when things get tough. Resilience allows us to enjoy our achievements and approach our goals realistically, which keeps us moving forward during hard times. It's not only about being strong; resilient people also use innovative strategies to handle life's challenges. Being ready and strong is essential when unexpected problems arise. Without resilience, we might feel overwhelmed and miss chances to grow personally. This chapter will examine the qualities that help successful people overcome tough times.

When you adopt a realistic mindset, setbacks start to look like minor detours instead of huge barriers. This chapter will show how realistic thinking can help you not only survive but also thrive in challenging situations.

Goal-setting is key to resilience, so we will look at the importance of setting achievable goals that lead to success. You'll learn how to break big dreams into smaller tasks, making it easier to see your progress. We'll also discuss how aligning your goals with your core values can motivate you to keep moving forward. Daily habits are essential, and we'll explore how creating supportive routines can keep you grounded and focused during uncertain times. Let's discover practical insights and strategies for building resilience and fostering realistic thinking, turning challenges into chances for growth.

## THE ART OF SETTING REALISTIC GOALS

Establishing achievable and meaningful goals is a key ingredient in building resilience. But why? The very nature of realistic and attainable goals helps prevent feelings of being overwhelmed and discouraged, which can often derail progress. Setting our sights on goals that are within reach acts as a buffer against stress. It's like having a road map; you might inevitably feel lost or overwhelmed without one.

That's why breaking down big dreams into manageable steps is key. Here's a funny example: Imagine trying to eat a whole cake in one bite—impossible, right? But slice by slice, it's much more doable. By dissecting larger aspirations into smaller tasks, you create a pathway where progress feels tangible and continuous. This approach makes your to-do list less overwhelming and maintains momentum over time.

Now, a common powerful tool for goal-setting that aligns well with this idea is the SMART criteria. SMART stands for specific, measurable, achievable, relevant, and time-bound. Applying these principles ensures that goals are well-defined and focused. It allows us to outline clearly what we want to achieve and map out how to get there. For example, rather than saying "I want to be healthier," a SMART goal would be "I will exercise for thirty minutes five times a week." This specificity makes it easier to track progress and stay motivated (Sutton, 2024).

Accomplishing steps is also about aligning them with personal values and priorities. As humans, staying motivated and happy while doing something that doesn't align with our core beliefs and values is very hard. This brings me to the question: Are you aware of your values and beliefs? Tough question? Don't worry—I got you. Below are some prompts to help you identify your core beliefs and values. You can write down your answers.

## PROMPTS FOR UNDERSTANDING YOUR CORE BELIEFS AND VALUES

When your goals resonate with what truly matters to you, they become more motivating. For example, if someone values family highly, their goals might revolve around creating more quality family time rather than simply advancing in a career that demands excessive hours away from home.

So, what are core beliefs and values? They are the foundational principles that guide your decisions, actions, and interactions with others. They shape how you perceive the world and influence what you prioritize in your life. Understanding these core beliefs and values helps you to align your goals with what genuinely matters to you, creating a sense of fulfillment and purpose. Below are some prompts to help you identify and understand your core beliefs better:

- What qualities do I admire in others?
- What actions make me feel proud of myself?
- What are the things I cannot compromise on?
- What values did I learn from my parents or guardians?
- How do I define success for myself?
- What causes or issues stir strong emotions in me?
- What do I believe is the purpose of life?
- How do I want to be remembered?

- What are my biggest fears, and what do they reveal about my values?
- What experiences have shaped my beliefs?
- In what ways do I feel I can make a positive impact?
- What do I truly enjoy doing that brings me joy and satisfaction?
- Who are my role models, and what values do they embody?
- What is the relationship between my spirituality and my values?
- How do I respond to challenges or setbacks in my life?
- What boundaries are important for me to maintain in relationships?

Thinking about these questions will help you find the beliefs and values that influence your decisions. For instance, you might discover that honesty is very important to you, leading you to a job in counseling or social work where you can help others openly and fairly. Someone else might realize that being creative makes them happy, pushing them to pursue art or come up with new solutions in their job. Knowing your values gives you a better view of your choices in life.

A good way to look into your central beliefs is to check your daily actions against these values regularly. You can ask yourself if your choices match what matters most to you. Making choices that don't align with your values might mean it's time to rethink your goals and commitments. This self-check helps you connect more deeply with who you are and can lead to a more genuine life.

Talking with friends or family can also help you understand your core beliefs. They might share thoughts or views that you haven't thought about. Hearing their views on your values can show you where you agree and disagree. These talks can lead to deeper thinking about why you believe what you do and how that shows in your actions. Consider how your beliefs have changed over time.

Experiences, education, and relationships can influence and shift your beliefs. Reflecting on these changes can show you that your values aren't fixed; they can grow and change as you live your life. This adaptability can lead to new opportunities and insights that enhance your understanding.

Finding your core beliefs and values can help you create a guide for living a satisfying life. This clarity can act like a compass, directing your everyday choices. This process can transform your daily habits and major life decisions into opportunities to connect with what is truly important to you. When your life aligns with your core beliefs, you may experience more peace, purpose, and happiness.

## LEARN TO CELEBRATE YOUR INCREMENTAL VICTORIES

One thing that can easily weigh us down and make it harder to keep going is being too hard on ourselves. This often happens when we have huge goals and never take the time to appreciate and celebrate the small victories along the way to achieving those bigger goals. It can cause a painful pattern of constantly feeling unhappy with our lives and, thus, also cause us to think of ourselves negatively despite having evident success.

To prevent that from happening again, let's try to drill into our minds the paramount importance of celebrating small victories. Each small achievement serves as positive reinforcement, boosting confidence and motivation. In therapeutic settings, for instance, recognizing minor achievements can significantly impact overall success (Wolmark, 2025). These victories act as stepping stones, paving the way toward larger ambitions while reinforcing the belief that bigger goals are within reach.

Psychologically, celebrating small wins releases dopamine, which enhances mood and encourages perseverance. It's like getting a high-five after each step taken during a marathon—you feel encouraged to keep going! Appreciating your progress helps you focus on how far you've come instead of what you still need to do. This boosts your confidence and makes it less likely that setbacks will discourage you.

It's also important to regularly check and adjust your goals. Life can change unexpectedly, so being flexible with your goals will keep them relevant. If a goal no longer makes sense or seems too hard because of new circumstances, rethinking it can reduce stress and open up opportunities for other important things.

Celebrating your achievements, no matter how small, helps fight negative thoughts by highlighting what you've accomplished instead of what you haven't. This can improve your self-esteem and build a stronger mindset by focusing on your strengths rather than on failures.

Finally, involving others in your goal-setting can make it more effective. Sharing your goals with trusted friends or family can provide support and accountability. They can encourage you, celebrate your successes, and help you stay focused when you face challenges. Knowing that someone believes in your ability to succeed can really help when times get tough.

## CREATING SUPPORTIVE ROUTINES

Building resilience through realistic thinking often means using structured habits that help your mind and body grow. One effective way to do this is by creating daily routines that bring stability. This isn't about being overly strict but about finding a steady rhythm that supports your well-being, especially when things are uncertain or changing.

Daily routines create a sense of predictability. In a world full of surprises, routines act as anchors, giving comfort through familiarity. They help create order when you can't control what's happening around you. This stability is crucial because it saves your mental energy, which would otherwise be used to decide what to do next. When your day has a clear pattern, it's easier to avoid chaos and reduce anxiety. Routines bring peace and focus, supporting you in tackling even the most challenging situations from a place of clarity (Selman & Dilworth-Bart, 2023).

Let's talk specifics: Habits that help growth include simple actions like waking up at the same time each day, exercising regularly, and taking time to think or write in a journal. Morning routines often have things like stretching or deep breathing, which can help make the day better. Drinking a glass of water after waking up also helps refresh the body and starts the day off right.

Physical activity, specifically, plays an essential role in routine formation. While it's true that developing such habits requires effort and time—from 18 to as many as 254 days to become automatic (Arlinghaus & Johnston, 2018)—the benefits are significant. Exercise releases endorphins, improving mood and mental clarity. Similarly, planning meals helps avoid decision fatigue related to dietary choices, fostering better nutrition without constant deliberation.

Many successful people believe their achievements come from solid routines. Think about athletes or business leaders who follow morning habits that get them ready for their day. These routines often include activities that help improve focus and productivity, like setting goals, meditating, or exercising. For instance, business owners might begin their day by reviewing their goals, then work in focused sessions with breaks in between to keep their energy up.

Routines also help manage stress. Having a consistent schedule not only helps personal growth but also protects against daily stresses. When routines reduce the number of choices you have to make each day, it decreases decision fatigue, allowing mental energy for other tasks. Planning meals or activities in advance means fewer last-minute decisions, which can lead to better choices and a clearer mind during the day. Additionally, sticking to a routine provides a structure that can be changed when needed, making it easier to adapt to new situations.

To make the most of routines, follow these steps: First, find key habits that match your goals, whether related to health, work, or leisure. Start small if needed, like writing in a journal for five minutes each morning or taking a short walk in the evening. Next, create a flexible plan that fits these habits into your daily life. Keep it practical; don't worry about being perfect, as occasional slip-ups won't stop your progress. Over time, these habits will become routines, leading to a steady and strong way of living.

## ACTIVELY BUILDING AN ENVIRONMENT FOR GROWTH

We thrive when we have healthy relationships in our personal and professional lives. You know the kind of people I'm talking about, the ones who remind you of your strengths and capabilities when you forget how awesome you are. Those supportive friends and family help you stay motivated to keep going. But it's not always easy to have this kind of support network, is it? That's why learning to create a nurturing environment will make a huge difference in our lives. It helps us build positive relationships that help us stay resilient. So, let's find out some helpful tips on things we can practice to start cultivating those strong and lasting bonds. These are people who encourage you to think realistically and promote mutual growth. They should inspire you and constructively challenge your thoughts.

## TIPS FOR STRENGTHENING YOUR SOCIAL SKILLS AND BUILDING A SUPPORTIVE NETWORK

To strengthen your relationships and expand your social network, you need to build your social skills. Practicing active listening can be particularly effective in connecting with others more deeply. This means making eye contact and truly engaging in conversations. Thoughtful responses show that you value what others have to say, which helps build trust. Additionally, asking open-ended questions can encourage people to share more about themselves, giving you a better understanding of their perspective. Always aim to validate their feelings; showing empathy is vital for forming meaningful bonds.

### *Connect With Others Who Have Shared Interests*

The first step is to find out what you like and what is important to you. Think about what you care about most. Once you know your interests, look for groups or communities where people with similar interests come together. This could be a book club, a professional group, or even starting your own hobby group.

Joining group activities is a great way to improve your social skills. You can join a sports team, participate in a volunteer project, or go to a workshop. Being part of a group helps everyone work together. When people aim for the same goal, it promotes teamwork and builds friendships. You create shared memories that connect everyone. Taking part in these activities teaches you about different personalities, which helps you deal with various social situations. Being involved with these groups can lead to rich experiences and valuable lessons, fostering a culture of growth together.

Getting involved in your community is a good way to meet new people. Attend events or join clubs that interest you. Meeting new people in your community can make you feel like you belong.

Engaging with different groups makes life more interesting and exposes you to new ideas.

### Set Healthy Boundaries

Setting healthy boundaries is a key ingredient for any good relationship to sprout (Nash, 2018). This means we have to recognize when to say no and express our needs openly. Clear boundaries show respect for ourselves and others, which in turn creates trust in our relationships. That's why it's essential to communicate what makes you comfortable or uncomfortable so that others understand your limits. When we respect our own boundaries, we encourage others to do the same. This not only helps us maintain balance in our lives but also prevents the emotional drain that often comes from overextending ourselves.

### Have a Positive and Grateful Attitude

Is it easy to be around someone who constantly complains and seldom ever shows gratitude for what's going well? It's not at all. This means that to attract positive relationships, we have to mindfully demonstrate gratitude for what we already have. Practicing gratitude in our relationships significantly strengthens our connections with others. A simple thank you for someone's effort or time goes a long way in showing appreciation. Noticing the contributions of others helps create a positive atmosphere and reinforces mutual respect. It doesn't have to be grand things; we can consider sending a quick message or writing a note of appreciation to leave a lasting impression. Acknowledging other people's strengths uplifts them and enriches our social interactions, making our network even more vibrant.

### Sharing Vulnerability

Sharing vulnerability can deepen bonds with others. When you open up about your challenges, you create space for others to share theirs as well. Authentic communication nurtures honesty and support, making you appear more relatable. These kinds of conversations can even lead to collaborations to overcome challenges, helping to establish a solid foundation of trust.

### Nurture a Positive Mindset

A positive mindset dramatically influences how you interact with others. Approaching social situations with enthusiasm and optimism tends to be contagious. Your good energy can draw others in, and a cheerful demeanor can help lift the spirits of those around you. Maintaining a can-do attitude encourages shared adventures, further enhancing connections with others.

### Recognize Social Cues

Being mindful of others' reactions can guide how you engage in conversation. Reading a room and adapting your approach based on social cues can lead to smoother interactions. If someone seems disinterested or uncomfortable, changing the subject or tone can help. This attentiveness demonstrates respect for their feelings and reinforces care in your relationships, ultimately leading to effective communication.

### Set Realistic Expectations

Setting realistic expectations can prevent disappointment in social interactions. It's important to understand that not every encounter will lead to a deep connection. Allow relationships to develop naturally without forcing them. Welcome the process of meeting new people and enjoy lighter interactions as growth opportunities.

### Take Initiative

Taking initiative in social settings is also a way to show your interest in others. Don't hesitate to reach out to someone, whether it's to arrange a coffee or organize an outing. Displaying enthusiasm and a willingness to invest time reinforces the value you place on the relationship. These actions can spark fun and memorable experiences that strengthen your bonds.

### Reflecting on Your Relationships

Regularly reflecting on your relationships enables you to assess your social health. Take time to evaluate which connections uplift you and which may be draining. Make conscious decisions to invest more in nurturing relationships that nourish you. This practice emphasizes the importance of surrounding yourself with those who share your values and aspirations.

### Practice Inclusivity

Practicing inclusivity in social interactions opens the door to more connections. Be mindful of including everyone in conversations and activities. Bridging gaps between different groups strengthens community ties and promotes collaboration. Showing kindness to people from various backgrounds can broaden your perspective and enhance your social skills.

### Share Laughter

Sharing laughter creates some of the strongest bonds in friendships. Embrace humor in your social interactions, as it lightens the mood and helps people connect. Sharing funny stories or experiences brings joy and leaves a lasting impression. Being around people who appreciate laughter nurtures a positive environment, allowing relationships to thrive.

### Seek Opportunities to Learn

Finally, look for ways to learn about social relationships. Read books, go to workshops, and join talks about building connections. Being curious about how to socialize can open your mind to new ideas. This focus on learning can improve your social skills and help you grow over time.

Having a mentor can provide valuable guidance and support based on their experiences. A mentor who thinks realistically and shows resilience can be a good example for you. They can share their knowledge, helping you handle challenges better. Mentors also encourage you to try new things and support you during tough times. Look for mentors in your network, someone you respect who has taken a similar path. Their insights can help you see new options and reassure you on your journey.

Joining support groups with peers can help you grow and strengthen your resilience. These groups, whether formed officially or among friends, give you a place to talk about your challenges, ideas, and successes. They provide support and feedback, helping you view your struggles and achievements from a different angle. Peer support promotes respect and understanding, making everyone feel appreciated. Activities like regular check-ins or group projects can make these networks more effective.

When building these support networks, focus on honesty and open communication. Clearly stating your expectations and needs helps build strong relationships, whether with mentors or peers. Checking in regularly on how support is shared ensures that the relationships are fair and valuable. Being empathetic and really listening can strengthen these connections, making everyone feel heard and supported.

## THE ROLE OF PATIENCE IN BUILDING HAPPY RELATIONSHIPS

Many times, the negative experiences we go through arise from the relational experiences we have with others. Without patience, negativity can overtake us like a storm. Thus, let's unearth some practical strategies to help us develop patience when things get tough. This way, we can overcome the setbacks we have in our relationships and not allow toxic thinking to rob us of the joy of experiencing growth and forgiveness in our relationships.

- **Become a patient listener:** Listening patiently is a part of nurturing relationships. When someone shares their thoughts or feelings, it is important to let them speak without interruption. Take, for example, a time when a friend comes to you after a tough day at work. Instead of rushing to offer solutions, you can simply listen as they vent their frustrations. You can nod and make simple comments like, "That sounds really hard." This simple act of patience allows them to feel heard and valued, and it opens the door for a deeper conversation later.
- **Be okay with giving others space or time:** Practicing patience can also mean giving others the time they need to understand their feelings. Say you notice your brother struggling with a decision about a job offer. He keeps second-guessing himself, and you sense his anxiety. Instead of pushing him for an answer, you can invite him to share his concerns. By saying something like, "Take your time. I'm here to listen," you create a space where he could think it through. He can unpack his thoughts and, by the end, feel more confident about his decision because he has processed everything out loud.
- **Be present:** In relationships, patience isn't only about letting people talk; it also means being present in those moments. We've all experienced a situation at a work or family gathering where someone shared a long story. Some people around the table might have looked at their phones, clearly bored. However, making an effort to engage, asking questions, and showing genuine interest can make that person feel respected, seen, and heard. This is how connections grow—by being fully engaged with one another.

- **Respect differences:** Understanding and accepting differences is another way to practice patience. If you have different views from someone, you might find yourself in discussions that get a bit heated. Rather than focusing on proving who's right, decide to practice patience. Whenever you disagree, take a step back, allowing each other to explain our perspectives fully. It feels refreshing, and it helps you comprehend each other better despite your differences. It strengthens relationships when everyone can speak openly without judgment.

- **Forgive and let go:** Patience also plays a role in forgiving mistakes, whether big or small. Instead of expressing anger, address those who hurt you calmly. This allows them to step back from the situation and offer an explanation without feeling attacked. Through patience and forgiveness, you resolve the issue and build a stronger working relationship.

- **Be okay with silence:** Sometimes, patience means allowing silence in conversations. It can feel awkward, but that pause often leads to deeper insights. For instance, during a heart-to-heart with a close friend, I stopped talking to let her reflect after sharing some challenging emotions. This space led her to express feelings she hadn't even realized were there. Those moments are when true understanding occurs, and they lead to stronger relationships.

- **Use encouraging language:** Language plays a significant role in how we express patience. Simple affirmations like "I see you" or "Take your time" can be incredibly powerful. Try incorporating these phrases into your conversations. A slight shift in how you communicate can change your relationships. You will start noticing that almost every time you meet someone halfway with understanding, you are both likely to walk away a little more connected. By holding space for those we care about,

> we create an atmosphere where they can share fears,
> dreams, and every little thought in between. That
> openness nurtures trust and honesty, essential ingredients
> for any meaningful relationship. With each act of
> patience, we allow others to grow and encourage
> ourselves to do the same.

Through patience, we learn that growth is often messy and takes time. Like planting flowers, we understand the importance of waiting for them to bloom, allowing time for roots to grow deeply. In many ways, being patient becomes an act of love. It shows that we value the relationship more than the momentary discomfort of waiting. Everyone has their own timeline for opening up, and it is important to honor this. Some may take longer to share their thoughts and feelings, and that's completely okay. Consistent support and understanding can build deeper connections over time. When you show patience, it demonstrates that you value the relationship, which fosters loyalty and trust.

## PRACTICAL EXERCISES FOR BUILDING RESILIENCE

Building resilience through realistic thinking is about strengthening our ability to move forward in the face of adversity. Engaging in specific exercises can enhance our resilience skills and prepare us for future challenges.

### *Build Resilience Through Mindfulness*

Adding mindfulness practices to our daily routines is a great way to build resilience. Mindfulness means focusing on the present moment without judging it. This is important because it helps us become more aware of ourselves, which can improve how we handle our emotions. For example, taking a moment each day to breathe deeply and check in with our feelings can calm our minds and help us respond to situations better. By practicing mindfulness, we learn to manage our reactions and reduce quick responses that often come from stress or anxiety.

When we encounter tough situations, mindfulness helps us stay calm. It lets us step back and observe our thoughts and feelings without getting overwhelmed. This awareness helps us identify what triggers our emotions. For example, if you know some situations make you angry or anxious, mindfulness helps you notice those feelings as they come up. This understanding gives you a chance to manage those emotions better, which builds your resilience. By being aware of how you react to stress, you can take steps to handle it effectively.

### Cognitive Restructuring for Positive Thinking

A key way to build resilience is through cognitive restructuring. This approach focuses on changing negative thoughts that many of us experience. Often, we get stuck in negative thinking, which makes it harder to deal with changes and challenges. Cognitive restructuring helps us spot and replace these harmful thoughts with more positive ones. For instance, if you think, *I'll never succeed at this*, cognitive restructuring encourages you to question that thought. You can ask yourself, *What proof do I have for this thought?* or *Is there a better way to look at this situation?*

This practice can help you change the way you think. For example, if you often doubt your ability to get things done, you can challenge that by remembering times you were successful. You create a healthier mindset by focusing on positive beliefs and letting go of unrealistic ones. These techniques are effective in changing negative thoughts and building resilience.

### Role-Playing to Prepare for Challenges

Role-playing scenarios can help build resilience. You can do it by simulating potential challenges or stressful situations. You can practice using adaptive coping strategies in a controlled environment.

This means you can think about difficult conversations or significant life changes and rehearse how you might handle them. By doing this, role-playing prepares us to anticipate obstacles before they happen.

For example, if you know you need to have a tricky conversation with a colleague, you can practice what you want to say. This helps you test out different approaches and develop problem-solving skills. A study suggests that using scripts and role-playing can help us express our fears and anxieties. When we practice this way, those fears can lose their power when we finally face them in real life. The more we prepare, the more resilient we become, as we build confidence in our ability to cope with various situations (Ackerman, 2017).

**Practical Application of Role-Playing**

To practice role-playing well, find specific situations that make you feel stressed or anxious. Write down the situation and think about how it might unfold. Create a script for yourself, including what you would say and how you would react. You can also practice this with a friend or family member who can give you help and feedback.

This practice can improve your communication skills. Approach role-playing with an open mind and a desire to learn. By putting yourself in imagined situations, you can prepare better for similar challenges in real life.

### *Nurture Healthy Positivity Through Gratitude Journaling*

Keeping a gratitude journal is a great way to focus on positive experiences and build a strong mindset. When you regularly write down things you are thankful for, it helps you stay positive. You might list simple things from your day, like enjoying a hot cup of coffee or laughing with a friend. Noticing these good moments, even if they seem small, teaches your mind to find joy even during tough times.

Writing about what you appreciate goes beyond just seeing the good; it helps you become emotionally stronger. Acknowledging the positives in your life can lessen the effects of negative events. A gratitude journal keeps track of happy moments you can reflect on when things get hard. This practice can improve your overall happiness and emotional strength. Research shows that practicing gratitude can lead to greater happiness and strong resilience (Rose, 2024).

It's easy to make gratitude journaling a daily habit. Pick a specific time each day, like just before bed or first thing in the morning, and write down three things you are thankful for that day. This practice helps you focus less on stress and more on what makes you happy.

### Strategies for Daily Mindfulness Integration

To seamlessly integrate mindfulness into daily life, you can start small. Start by spending a few minutes each day being present. You can try mindful breathing when you wake up or during your breaks at work. Focus on your breath, pay attention to how your body feels, and let go of distractions. Over time, these short moments can grow into longer activities, like guided meditations or relaxing walks in nature where you notice what's around you.

Another way to improve mindfulness is through mindful eating. Take time to enjoy each bite of your food. Notice the tastes, textures, and smells. This practice helps you slow down and appreciate your meal instead of hurrying through it. Simple moments like these can greatly improve your emotional strength and overall health.

### Building a Routine Around Cognitive Techniques

To use cognitive restructuring effectively, try to make it a part of your daily life. Keep a journal to write down negative thoughts as they happen. For each thought, find ways to question it. Ask yourself if these thoughts are true, and write down what you find. Over time, this can become a habit that helps you think more positively.

Use affirmations as another way to change your thinking. Write positive statements about what you can do and what you want to achieve. For example, if you want to feel more confident, tell yourself, "I can reach my goals." Repeat these affirmations often to help build a positive attitude.

## SUMMING UP

Setting realistic goals is like having a reliable roadmap for building resilience. We learned how to create achievable goals and break them down into manageable tasks without feeling overwhelmed. When we take a proactive approach to resilience building, we set ourselves up for overcoming the inevitable storms that come our way. All the elements we discussed are building blocks of resilience. To further cement a strong, unstoppable mindset, the next chapter will guide us with tips for achieving that and mastering the art of sustainably thriving amidst difficult or negative situations.

# STEP 7: REDEFINE SUCCESS

What is success, and why should we redefine it? It's because, at times, there's something fundamentally marred about how we sometimes view success. That distorted perspective of how we view success can slowly eat away at our mental health unless we correct what's wrong. This entails having healthy and realistic expectations for what true success is. The concept of redefining success means looking beyond traditional things like money and status. Nowadays, many people go after these symbols of success, only to feel more confused when they achieve their goals. It's easy to get caught up in what society thinks, but what if we took a moment to think about what success really means to us? Instead of focusing on outside rewards, we could concentrate on being true to ourselves. This chapter encourages you to think about that. We'll see how being authentic can bring you more happiness than any award or title.

You will find stories of people who have defined success in their own ways. Some prioritize family time over job promotions, while others prefer creative expression over social standing. Their experiences offer valuable lessons. As you think about your own life, you can identify your key values and create your personal definition of success. When your goals align with your values, your life becomes more fulfilling, and new opportunities come your way. We will also talk about achieving work and work-life balance or contributing positively to our community. Let's start this adventure together, where real success means being true to yourself.

## A NEW DEFINITION OF SUCCESS

Isn't it sad that we often gauge success based on wealth and status in today's society? Many people associate a high income or a prestigious title with achievement. Despite reaching these financial heights or receiving accolades, a great number still feel unfulfilled. This sense of dissatisfaction stems from the fact that traditional measures of success generally overlook personal values and passions. It's important to understand that success is not a universal concept; it varies for each individual. When we try to live up to societal expectations, we can end up feeling empty and disconnected from our true selves.

### Craft Your Own Definition of Success

What would happen if we could create our own definitions of success that truly reflect who we are? To start this process, you can consider crafting a *personalized success manifesto*. Don't worry, this idea isn't a mere fancy thought; it's an authentic way to find true happiness in life. A success manifesto is like a personal blueprint that outlines what success means to you. It's an empowering tool that can help guide your actions and decisions based on your own values and priorities. Crafting one can be a fun and rewarding experience, especially if you engage with it like an adventure. The process starts with self-reflection—taking time to think deeply about your feelings and beliefs to find out what matters most to you. This means you have to ask yourself what you care about in life.

For instance, you might realize that spending time with your family is more important than having a nice office. Or you may find that being able to create art every day means more to you than getting promoted at work. After figuring out these values, the next step is to set goals that match what really matters to you. This way, the choices you make feel true to who you are and give your life meaning. Below are guidelines that can help in creating your own success manifesto:

1. **Begin with your values**: Jot down what truly matters to you. Is it creativity, family, health, adventure, or something else?
2. **Make it visual**: Grab some colorful markers and a large sheet of paper. Sketch out your values and what they look like for you. A visual representation can bring your ideas to life!
3. **Write affirmations**: Create positive statements that resonate with your values. For example, "I am successful when I nurture my creativity" or "I find success in building strong relationships."
4. **Set clear goals**: Outline specific and achievable goals based on your values and affirmations. For instance, if family time is essential, your goal could be, "I will have dinner with my family three times a week."

Keep this process light and enjoyable. Listen to uplifting music while you work on your manifesto, or invite friends to join you for a brainstorming session. Encourage open discussions where everyone shares their ideas and supports one another. Ask questions like, "What does success look like for you?" or "How can we help each other achieve our goals?"

Once your manifesto starts taking shape, continue refining it. Don't hesitate to revisit and change it as you grow. Life is full of surprises, and you may find that your definition of success evolves over time. Be flexible! Embrace the process of discovering new insights and adapting your goals accordingly. Use the manifesto as a daily reminder. You can hang it somewhere visible, such as above your workspace or on your fridge. This way, it serves as a touchstone, guiding you back whenever you feel lost or overwhelmed. Every time you read it, let it inspire you to take steps toward your version of success.

Include enjoyable activities that match your beliefs. If being creative matters to you, host a craft night with friends. If adventure is important to you, plan fun weekend trips or try new hobbies that challenge you. This approach to achieving success focuses on enjoying who you are and what you love, turning your journey into something fun instead of just a list of tasks.

Think about how to celebrate every win. Treat yourself to your favorite dessert when you reach a goal or plan a day out after finishing a big project. Acknowledging your achievements keeps you motivated and shows you that you're on the right path.

Next, spend time regularly reflecting on your progress. Set aside time each week or month to see if your actions match your beliefs. Ask yourself questions like, or *Am I making choices that help me reach my goals?* This practice helps you stay responsible for your journey. Also, share your success goals with supportive people. Having a cheering team makes it more enjoyable to accomplish your goals. They can encourage you and keep you on track, which often leads to better success. The bonus advantage of talking about your goals is that it allows others to share theirs, creating a supportive community.

Maintain a positive attitude toward the failures during your journey. When things don't go as planned, treat them as opportunities to learn instead of setbacks. Ask yourself, *What can I learn from this?* or *How can I change my plan?* The path to success may have challenges, and viewing them as lessons can make the journey easier.

Feel free to update your goals whenever you reach new milestones or go through big changes in your life. Life changes, and your definition of success should, too. Keeping your goals relevant to your current self is crucial for staying happy and focused. Imagine what you will look like when you've achieved your version of success. Close your eyes and picture it. How does that feel? Keeping this image in mind can motivate you as you pursue your goals. Celebrate your uniqueness on this path. There's no need to compare; your success is just for you. Own it, and let it lead you to a more vibrant life. By focusing on what energizes you and aligns with your beliefs, you create a rewarding life that feels true to who you are. Each step taken in line with your goals gets you closer to a happier and more authentic life.

## THE MANY FACES OF SUCCESS

As we talk about success, let's consider unconventional success stories. These stories highlight the diversity of what success can look like in various contexts. For some people, success may mean achieving a balance between work and life. They might decide to leave a high-stress job to focus on a healthier lifestyle. Some seek creative fulfillment, such as artists and writers who prioritize self-expression over societal approval and prestige. Many people still find joy in dedicating their lives to helping their communities, emphasizing the importance of making a positive impact over earning a hefty paycheck. These narratives serve as reminders that success can manifest in multiple forms, going well beyond mere monetary gain.

Personal stories help us rethink success and encourage us to look inside ourselves to find the courage to follow our true paths. When we examine our feelings, we can ignore society's expectations and figure out what we really want. It takes bravery to go against what others expect and to take less common routes. When we focus on what truly drives them instead of outside pressures, they often find that their idea of success makes them happier and improves their lives.

Many people's life stories show how people have gone against social norms to chase their passions. For example, some people leave high-paying jobs to volunteer and work on community projects that bring them joy. While these choices may seem unusual to those who only value money, for those making these decisions, the happiness they gain is more valuable than any paycheck.

## KENDRA'S SUCCESS STORY

Kendra always felt confined in her 9-to-5 job. Every morning, she would sit at her desk, staring at spreadsheets, feeling a tug in her chest. *This isn't who I am*, she often thought. One day, during her lunch break, she overheard a colleague discussing a small business they had started from scratch. The excitement in their voice sparked something within Kendra. "What if I could do that?" she wondered, her mind racing with possibilities.

That night, Kendra stayed up late, sketching out a plan for her own business. She loved baking and often made treats for her friends and family. *Why not turn this passion into something more?* she thought, her heart racing with the thrill of the idea. The next morning, she boldly walked into her boss's office. "I need to talk to you about my role here," she said, her voice steady.

She explained her desire to leave and pursue her baking business full-time. Her boss raised an eyebrow in surprise. "You're giving up a steady paycheck for... cupcakes?" he asked, bewildered. Kendra nodded, unde-terred. "It's more than cupcakes. It's my dream." The conversation ended with her resignation, and she felt lighter than air as she walked out.

Her first few weeks were both exciting and challenging. Kendra set up a small kitchen in her home and started experimenting with recipes. *What if I add a pinch of salt to the chocolate cake?* she mused, mixing batter with a sense of purpose. Friends encouraged her, often stopping by to taste her creations. "You should sell these!" they said, their mouths full of cookies. Kendra beamed at the compliments, but she still had doubts.

One day, when she felt overwhelmed, she called her old colleague for advice. "It's scary stepping into the unknown," she admitted. Her friend laughed. "Of course it is! But remember, it's your path. Don't let fear knock you back down." This pep talk gave Kendra the boost she needed. She rolled up her sleeves, wrote a business plan, and set up a social media account. "If I'm going to do this, I need to be seen," she said.

As time passed, she gained a following. People loved her creations, and each like on her photos felt like validation. One Saturday, she decided to host a pop-up shop at a local market. It was a risk, but Kendra was ready. "I can do this," she repeated under her breath, setting up her booth filled with colorful cupcakes and cookies. The sun shone bright as she arranged the treats, and curious customers soon began to arrive.

"These look amazing!" one woman said, picking up a bright pink cupcake. Kendra smiled, feeling pride swell in her chest. The day was a whirlwind of baking and chatting. By the time the market closed, she was exhausted but thrilled. "I sold out!" she exclaimed over the phone to her family that night. They celebrated her success, reminding her of how far she'd come.

Kendra's leap of faith inspired many of her friends. They began sharing their own dreams and aspirations they had put aside, encouraging one another to pursue what truly made them happy. "If Kendra can do it, why can't I?" they said, making plans to follow their passions, whether it was painting, writing, or starting a podcast. Kendra had opened a door for others to walk through.

Weeks transformed into months, and Kendra's small business blossomed. She collaborated with local cafés, providing them with her baked goods. "This is just the beginning," she told herself as she brewed a pot of coffee one crisp morning, thinking about expanding her menu. Kendra learned to juggle many hats: baker, marketer, and accountant. It was hard work, but as she mixed dough in her kitchen, she felt a spark in her heart.

Challenges arose. There were days the oven broke down or the frosting didn't turn out right. "What am I doing?" she sighed one evening, feeling doubt creep back in. She remembered that her move from the corporate world to running her own business took courage. "This is a journey," she reminded herself, flipping through photos of success.

Kendra kept pushing through. She focused on her love for baking, using those struggles as fuel to keep moving forward. Her following grew, and soon, she started hosting baking classes online. "I want to share my passion," she announced in one of the videos, her energy contagious. The comments flooded in, and people joined from different regions, eager to learn.

As she taught, Kendra reflected on her journey, realizing she was no longer just an employee; she was an entrepreneur living her dream. Friends reached out for tips and advice. "You inspire me," one said over coffee, excitement dancing in her eyes. Kendra smiled, glad her story encouraged others to pursue their own paths, showing them that success can look different than traditional jobs.

All these moments solidified Kendra's belief that life doesn't have to fit into a box. Each success, from a new recipe to a class full of eager students, reinforced the idea that everyone's journey is unique. With every cupcake crafted, every student engaged, she felt a sense of fulfillment that no 9-to-5 could ever provide.

Kendra's story circulated among friends and family, inspiring more than just her immediate circle. Strangers began sharing her posts, and her little business turned into something bigger than she had ever imagined. She launched a website, expanded her offerings, and even began catering for events. Each new venture filled her with energy and excitement.

Many people started reaching out, eager to learn more about her business journey. Kendra happily shared her story, not just about baking but about taking risks and following one's passion. "It's about more than just business," she often said. "It's about living a life true to who you are." Her message resonated, and she dedicated time to mentoring others, hoping to light the fire in them just as she had discovered her own.

Kendra realized that success was not merely about money but about fulfilling her dream and inspiring others in the process. As she baked, taught, and inspired, her fear of the unknown slowly diminished, replaced by the joy of what she had created and the realization that chasing passion was the true recipe for happiness and success.

## THE VALUE OF QUIET VICTORIES

While society tends to celebrate grand, public accomplishments, the quieter victories are equally noteworthy. For instance, a person choosing to spend more time nurturing close family bonds instead of working late hours is redefining success in a way that aligns with their true values, just like how Kendra redefined her success to mean working for herself and no longer basking in a false sense of security of having the same job that didn't allow her to live a fulfilling life. This choice is far more meaningful than only attaining a huge salary.

This means we must learn to let go of comparing ourselves to others. As you move toward your unique definition of success, focus on your own path without being distracted by others' achievements. Everyone's journey is different, and drawing inspiration from diverse experiences can greatly expand your understanding of the possibilities that exist.

## LONG-TERM STRATEGIES FOR GROWTH

Adaptability means being willing to change and grow. This means we have to now regularly check in on our goals and be open to new opportunities that fit what we care about at different times in our lives. As we move through various experiences and situations, our interests can shift. This change can affect what we want to achieve. It's important to take time to look at your personal goals regularly to see if they match your current passions and who you are becoming.

For example, you might start your career in a job that excites you, but over time, your interests may change. This change can feel scary because it may seem like a big decision. However, it's a chance to match your career goals with what you now enjoy. Being adaptable in your pursuits can lead to personal happiness and keep you headed toward success by ensuring that your aims reflect your true self.

## TRACK YOUR PROGRESS

Having the right tools can help you keep track of your growth and set realistic goals. Writing in a journal allows you to record your experiences, challenges, and successes. This process can reveal patterns in your behavior and help you see areas where you might need to focus more effort. Digital apps can be incredibly helpful for organization. Apps can set reminders, track deadlines, and show your progress visually. Whether you choose a productivity app or one focused on mental wellness, these tools help you stay organized and motivated.

There are many apps available to help you track your progress. These apps vary in features and purposes, so you can choose the ones that best fit your needs. Here are ten suggested apps you might find useful:

1. **Trello:** This app helps you organize tasks visually. You can create boards for different projects, add cards for tasks, and move them as you progress.
2. **Habitica:** This app gamifies your habit tracking. You create an avatar and earn rewards for completing tasks, making progress fun and encouraging.
3. **Notion:** This versatile app combines notes, databases, and task management. You can customize it to fit your tracking needs.
4. **Todoist**: A straightforward task manager that allows you to create to-do lists. You can set due dates and prioritize tasks easily.
5. **MyFitnessPal:** If health is a focus, this app tracks your food intake and exercise. It helps you monitor your habits and stay on target with your fitness goals.
6. **Strides:** This app allows you to set specific goals and track your progress daily. You can add reminders and celebrate your achievements.
7. **Google Keep:** A note-taking app that lets you jot down quick ideas or reminders. You can organize notes by labels and colors for easy access.
8. **Journey:** A journaling app that encourages reflection. You can write entries, add photos, and even track your mood over time.
9. **Forest:** This productivity app helps you stay focused by growing a virtual tree while you work. If you leave the app, the tree dies, motivating you to stay on task.
10. **MindMeister:** A mind Mapping tool to visualize your thoughts and ideas. You can create maps that help organize your thoughts and plan projects.

Using these tools can provide a strong foundation for managing your goals and maintaining motivation. They help with organization and encourage accountability. Seeing your progress can be a significant boost to keep going.

As shared earlier, mentors can offer valuable guidance and share their experiences. They provide a different viewpoint during uncertain times. Having someone to talk to about your dreams can help you gain clarity and confidence. A good mentor encourages you to stretch your limits and keeps you accountable for your goals.

To make the most of these tools, start by deciding which method works best for you—journaling, using an app, or seeking a mentor. Make it a regular practice to update your progress. Set clear and achievable goals that help you move forward. Regularly check in on your strategies to see if they still fit your needs, and be sure to recognize and celebrate every milestone you reach.

### *Case Studies on Adaptability*

Let's look at some examples that highlight how being adaptable can lead to success. Consider Claire. She started her career in marketing because she was passionate about it. However, after a few years, she discovered her interests had shifted toward technology. Instead of staying stuck in marketing, Claire decided to embrace lifelong learning. She took online tech courses and attended workshops. This allowed her to transition into a new role in technology while still keeping the skills she developed in marketing. Her ability to adapt not only led her to a satisfying career but also showed her resilience in a changing environment.

Then there is John, who initially worked in corporate finance. He chose this path because he thought it was what he was supposed to do. Over time, he realized that he was more interested in education. By accepting this change, John created a niche for himself as a financial educator, merging his finance background with his passion for teaching others. Both Claire's and John's stories emphasize the importance of remaining true to your evolving interests while being mindful of the core values that guide them.

### Celebrate Your Milestones

Noticing and celebrating your milestones is key to sustaining energy and momentum over the long haul. Each milestone you reach shows the hard work you've put in. Celebrating these achievements can give you a boost and reinforce the idea that you are moving forward. Whether you land a job, learn a new skill, or finish a difficult project, celebrating these achievements reinforces your belief in your abilities.

You can celebrate your milestones in small but meaningful ways. It doesn't have to be extravagant. Maybe treat yourself to your favorite meal, enjoy a day at a spa, or spend time with friends and family. These celebrations serve as reminders of your hard-won accomplishments and help to inspire continued effort. Focusing on your achievements can make it easier to handle setbacks and keep a positive outlook.

Celebrating accomplishments not only encourages you but also builds confidence. Each time you recognize what you have done, you create a positive memory you can draw on during tough times. This helps you face challenges with a fresh mindset, filled with optimism. This practice also nurtures a greater appreciation for your journey. Instead of only focusing on your end goals, celebrating milestones creates a balanced approach that honors your efforts along the way. It reminds you that growth is a journey filled with both triumphs and challenges.

## INSPIRE OTHERS THROUGH YOUR JOURNEY

Sharing your story can be an incredible way to inspire others along this path. Just like what we saw in Kendra's story, when you open up about your personal experiences with honesty, it gives others the courage to pursue their dreams despite past struggles or failures. Similar to how lanterns light pathways on dark nights, authentic storytelling guides and reassures us that we're not alone in our quest for fulfillment. By being vulnerable, we create connections and build a supportive community, fostering a shared sense of purpose.

You may be unsure about how to start sharing your personal experiences. A good way to begin is by picking moments in your life where you showed determination and ended up with surprising successes. Think about times when being true to yourself led to important changes. These stories often contain useful lessons that others can relate to. They offer hope and show that challenges can become stepping stones for future success. Sharing isn't about bragging; it's a chance to help others learn from your experiences and reflect on their own journeys.

Looking back at your past is important, but considering your future matters, too. A strong way to do this is by writing a letter to your future self. This activity can capture what you want right now and help guide your choices ahead. Picture yourself five years from now. What would you appreciate about the path you are taking today? Writing down your dreams, worries, and thoughts helps you create space for reflecting on yourself and keeping your goals alive. It's like planting seeds for your future based on what you want today. Over time, as you read these letters again, you'll see how much you've changed and how your dreams have evolved. This reflection can help you stay in touch with your true self. Writing down advice or encouragement for your future self can remind you that you can shape your own story.

### The Importance of Lifelong Learning

Lifelong learning is essential for personal growth. It means being curious and willing to change and improve yourself. This attitude can inspire others to start their own paths of development. Each new skill you learn, every book you read, and meaningful conversation you have adds to who you are becoming. Lifelong learning keeps us engaged and open-minded, reminding us there is always something new to discover. While there are no strict rules for embracing learning, it helps to see each experience as unique yet part of a bigger picture of knowledge. This thinking encourages ongoing change and motivates those around you to push beyond their limits and achieve more than they thought possible.

### The Power of Personal Stories

Our personal stories have great power, especially when they include moments of overcoming challenges. These stories can inspire hope and strength by showing how problems can become chances to grow. Think about times when you faced difficulties and emerged stronger, smarter, or more determined. By sharing these stories, you show the strength we all have inside. These experiences can help others see that challenges are not just obstacles. Instead, they can be seen as steps toward success. The lessons learned from tough times can help others as they deal with their own challenges without losing sight of what they want to achieve.

Remember a time when you faced a big challenge. Think about how you felt, what you did, and what happened in the end. By sharing this story, you highlight your journey and offer valuable advice to others in similar situations. They can realize they are not alone in their struggles and that growth often comes from tackling problems directly. Each story of strength you tell adds to our understanding of what it means to be human. It can build a sense of community, showing that everyone faces difficulties, but our reactions make all the difference.

### Encouraging Others Through Your Narrative

Your experiences can be incredibly empowering for others. When you share the lessons learned during tough times, you not only enlighten them but also inspire hope. People often feel encouraged to forge ahead when they hear how someone else faced their fears or navigated uncertainties. Highlighting the positive changes that followed difficult periods can provide encouragement to those who may be feeling stuck.

Encourage others to embrace their own stories by sharing yours in a relatable way. You might mention a personal setback and how you approached it. Describe the steps you took to overcome the issue, the support you received, and how you found clarity along the way. This approach allows others to see that it is acceptable to experience hardship and that it is possible to emerge from it with newfound strength. It emphasizes that struggles do not define us; they can shape us into better versions of ourselves. When you frame your challenges as part of your journey toward growth, you help others understand that they, too, can turn their obstacles into opportunities.

### Creating a Legacy Through Storytelling

Storytelling helps create a lasting impact. Your experiences, both good and bad, can be shared with future generations. Sharing these stories connects your experiences with others who might learn from them. This responsibility encourages you to think more and share what you have learned. When you tell your stories, you add to our shared human experience. Each story contributes to a larger understanding of the challenges and successes people face. It shows that, despite our differences, we are all connected. This connection can inspire people to learn from your journey and share their own stories, creating a legacy of strength and hope for those who come after us. Storytelling opens up chances for conversation and connection, leading to better understanding and empowerment.

## SUMMING UP

We've dug deep into what success really means. Indeed, success is not about following the crowd or chasing after what we're told should make us happy. Instead, it's all about finding what makes you tick and sticking with it. When we focus on aligning our goals with our true selves and values, that's where true satisfaction comes from. We've heard stories of people who went against the grain—choosing happiness over high paychecks or prioritizing family over job titles— and they found success in their own unique ways. Their journeys remind us that success is personal, not something you can measure with just numbers or external approval.

As we wrap up, remember to always stay open to change and regularly check in with what genuinely matters to you. This path isn't always easy, but when you let go of comparisons and fully embrace your individuality, life becomes incredibly rewarding. So, think about what truly makes you happy, and let's redefine success on your terms for a richer, more fulfilling life.

# CONCLUSION

Congratulations on reaching the end of this part of your journey! You've taken a brave step in tackling the negativity that often clouds our potential, and by doing so, you've equipped yourself with new tools to reshape your thoughts and goals. It's crucial to remember that negativity and self-doubt aren't simply hurdles; they're signals pointing toward areas ripe for growth, and with the right approach, they can become transformative forces in our lives.

You've learned throughout this book that whatever we focus on—be it desirable or undesirable—grows. It's easy to get caught in the cycle of negative thinking, where worrying about potential problems becomes second nature. But now, you have the skills to shift that focus onto what you truly want to achieve. Instead of letting doubts dictate your actions, you're ready to use them as stepping stones, guiding you to a path more aligned with who you are and what you aspire to become.

Being negative is a habit that can feel strangely comfortable. It's familiar territory for many of us, making the transition to optimism seem daunting. But naive optimism isn't the goal here. We've talked about the importance of having practical plans to support positive thinking, ensuring that your optimism is not only hopeful but also grounded and actionable. You deserve a life filled with purpose and possibility, and nurturing an optimistic mindset is critical to achieving that.

It's okay if you don't feel there yet. Change doesn't happen overnight. But I want you to know that you have everything you need to thrive using the strategies outlined in this book. You've already shown remarkable resolve in reaching this point, and there's no limit to how much further you can go. The world is full of opportunities waiting for you to seize them. As you go forward, keep these insights close, and don't hesitate to revisit any chapter as needed. Each page holds nuggets of wisdom that can illuminate your path whenever you're feeling lost or overwhelmed.

Remember, you're never alone in this journey. Many others have walked similar paths and found great success in flipping their narratives from negativity to empowerment. I'd love to hear about your journey. Your success story could inspire someone else who feels trapped in their negative thoughts. If you have the time and feel inclined, please leave a review of this book. Share your experiences, highs, lows, breakthroughs, and revelations. Your words might be the encouragement someone else needs to begin their transformation.

Now, it's time for action. Don't wait another day to put into practice what you've learned. Start with the seven steps we've discussed. Pick one small thing you can do today that will initiate change. Your progress may start with baby steps, but even tiny movements forward count as momentum. Consistency is key, so as you move into this next phase, keep going back to the book. Let it be a resource and a guide as you navigate challenges and celebrate wins along the way.

In closing, here's something vital to remember: Your self-doubt isn't your enemy—it's your greatest tool for building a life of success and authenticity. Embrace it, understand it, and let it teach you. Every doubt carries a lesson, and as you learn, you'll find yourself growing in ways you never imagined possible. Trust in the process and trust in yourself.

As you step away from this book and back into the world, keep these sentiments in mind. You're capable of incredible things, and now you have the tools to fully uncover and harness that potential. Keep pushing forward, stay curious, and always be kind to yourself. This is just the beginning, and I can't wait to see all you accomplish. Remember, the road to an enriched life is traveled one step at a time, so keep stepping forward with confidence and determination.

Thank you for choosing this book as part of your journey and for trusting me to guide you through these concepts. I hope it has been as rewarding for you as it was for me to write. Here's to using negativity as a catalyst for positive change and living a life that genuinely reflects who you are. Go out there and unleash your full potential— you have everything within you to make it happen!

# REFERENCES

Ackerman, C. E. (2017, March 20). *Twenty-five CBT techniques and worksheets for cognitive behavioral therapy.* PositivePsychology.com. https://positivepsychology.com/cbt-cognitive-behavioral-therapy-techniques-worksheets

AH Admin, 2022. (2022, June 27). *How stress and worrying affect your body.* Avail Hospital Lake Charles. https://www.availhospitals.com/how-stress-and-worrying-affect-your-body/

Arlinghaus, K. R., & Johnston, C. A. (2018). The importance of creating habits and routine. *American Journal of Lifestyle Medicine, 13*(2), 142–144. https://www.ncbi.nlm.nih.gov/pmc/articles/PMC6378489/

Carville, C. (2024). *Setting healthy boundaries in relationships.* Resiliencelab.us. https://www.resiliencelab.us/thought-lab/healthy-boundaries

Charlie Health Team. (2023, October 27). *CBT journaling can help you deal with negative thoughts.* Charlie Health. https://www.charliehealth.com/post/cbt-journaling

Nash, J. (2018). *How to set healthy boundaries & build positive relationships.* Positive Psychology. https://positivepsychology.com/great-self-care-setting-healthy-boundaries/

Raypole, C. (2020, March 31). *Repressed emotions: Finding and releasing them.* Healthline. https://www.healthline.com/health/repressed-emotions

Robinson, L., Smith, M., & Segal, J. (2018, November 3). *How to stop worrying and end anxious thoughts.* HelpGuide.org. https://www.helpguide.org/mental-health/anxiety/how-to-stop-worrying

Rose, M. (2024, June 10). *Self-help strategies: Rose behavioral health's guide to personal wellness.* Rose Behavioral Health. https://www.rosebehavioralhealth.com/self-help-strategies-rose-behavioral-healths-guide-to-personal-wellness/

Selman, S. B., & Dilworth-Bart, J. E. (2023). Routines and child development: a systematic review. *Journal of Family Theory and Review, 1*(1). https://onlinelibrary.wiley.com/doi/full/10.1111/jftr.12549

Sutton, J. (2024, December 12). *The importance, benefits, and value of goal setting.* Positive Psychology. https://positivepsychology.com/benefits-goal-setting/

Wolmark, M. (2025, January 13). *The importance of tracking small wins in ABA therapy.* Goldenstepsaba.com; Golden Steps ABA. https://www.goldenstepsaba.com/resources/the-importance-of-tracking-small-wins-in-aba-therapy

# ABOUT THE AUTHOR

Joseph Vale is a New York-based author and personal development strategist dedicated to helping individuals harness the power of their thoughts to achieve authentic growth and success. Growing up in the fast-paced environment of New York City, Joseph faced high-pressure expectations and frequent self-doubt. Despite excelling in his early career, he struggled with perfectionism and the unrealistic standards set by toxic positivity. This personal experience ignited his passion for understanding the interplay between negativity, self-doubt, and success. With years of experience exploring mental health strategies and leading discussions around personal growth, Joseph has guided countless individuals to reframe their self-doubt and unlock their potential. His hands-on work with professionals, students, and creatives led him to discover a gap in traditional self-help narratives: the suppression of negative emotions.

Joseph's debut book, *Harness Negative Thinking: 7 Steps to Turn Self-Doubt Into Success Without Toxic Positivity,* combines practical advice with a relatable, empowering approach to challenge outdated self-help norms. It offers readers a realistic and actionable path to personal growth by embracing, rather than avoiding, their inner struggles. When he's not writing or advocating for mental wellness, Joseph can often be found playing basketball with friends, a sport he credits for teaching him discipline, teamwork, and perseverance. He is deeply committed to creating actionable strategies that resonate with people from all walks of life, showing that success doesn't require silencing your inner critic but learning how to work with it. Join Joseph Vale as he redefines personal development and helps readers turn their doubts into strengths, unlocking a path to lasting success and authentic growth.

# THANK YOU FOR BEING HERE

I just want to take a moment to say—from the bottom of my heart—
**thank you** for choosing this book.

You had plenty of options, but something in this message resonated
with you. And the fact that you stuck with it all the way to the end?
That means everything.

This book wasn't just written—it was lived. And if even one page
helped shift something in your thinking, calm your mind, or make
you feel a little less alone in the chaos, then it's done its job.

Before you go, I'd love to ask you a small favor.

If this book meant something to you—if you underlined a sentence,
took a deep breath, or whispered "yes" at any point—would you
consider leaving a quick review?

Even just a sentence or two helps other readers find this work. And it
helps me continue showing up, creating the kind of books that actually meet you where you are.

Your voice matters. I'd be honored to hear it.

—Joseph Vale

**>> Leave a review on Amazon <<: Scan me**